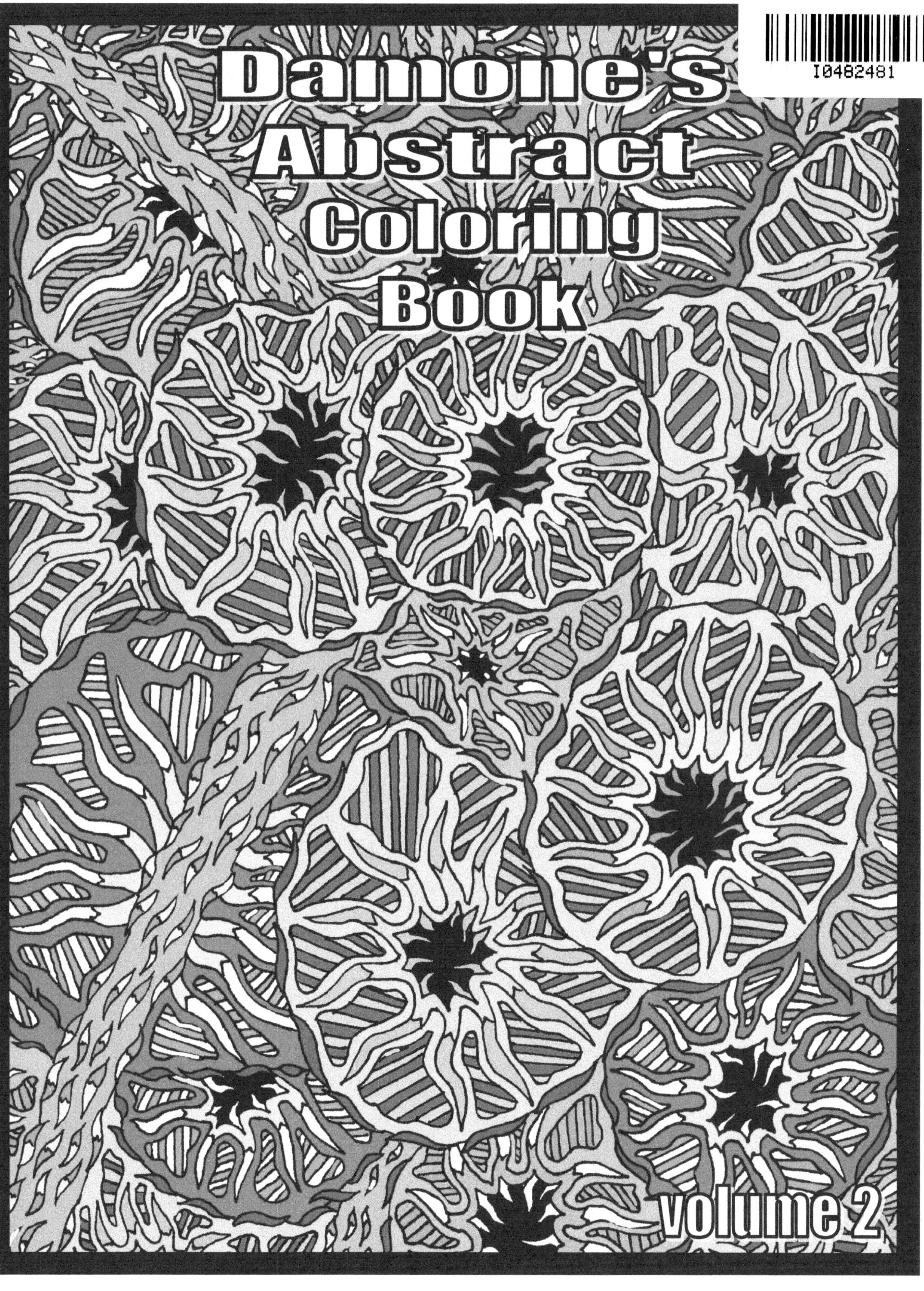
Damone's
Abstract
Coloring
Book
volume 2

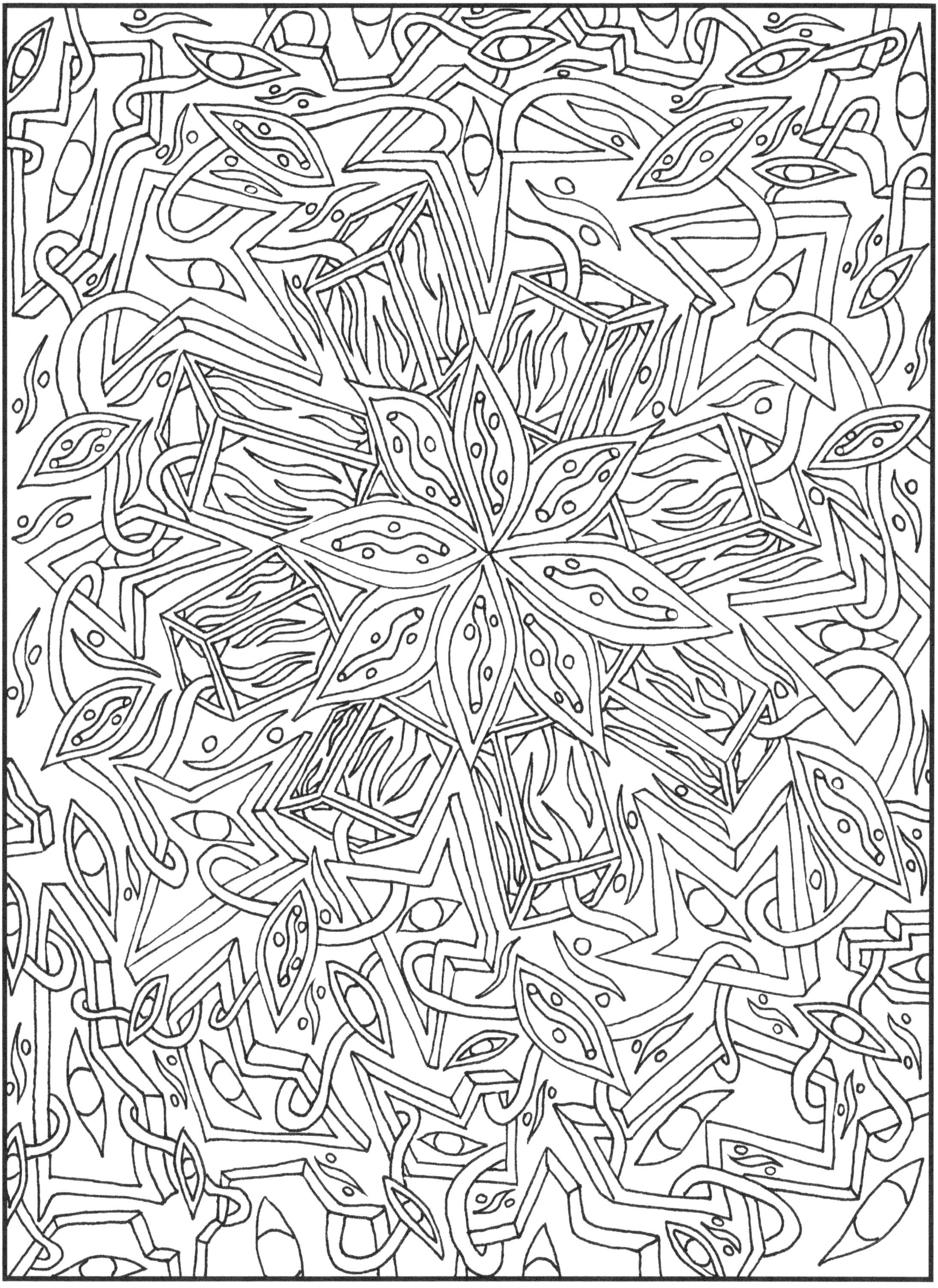

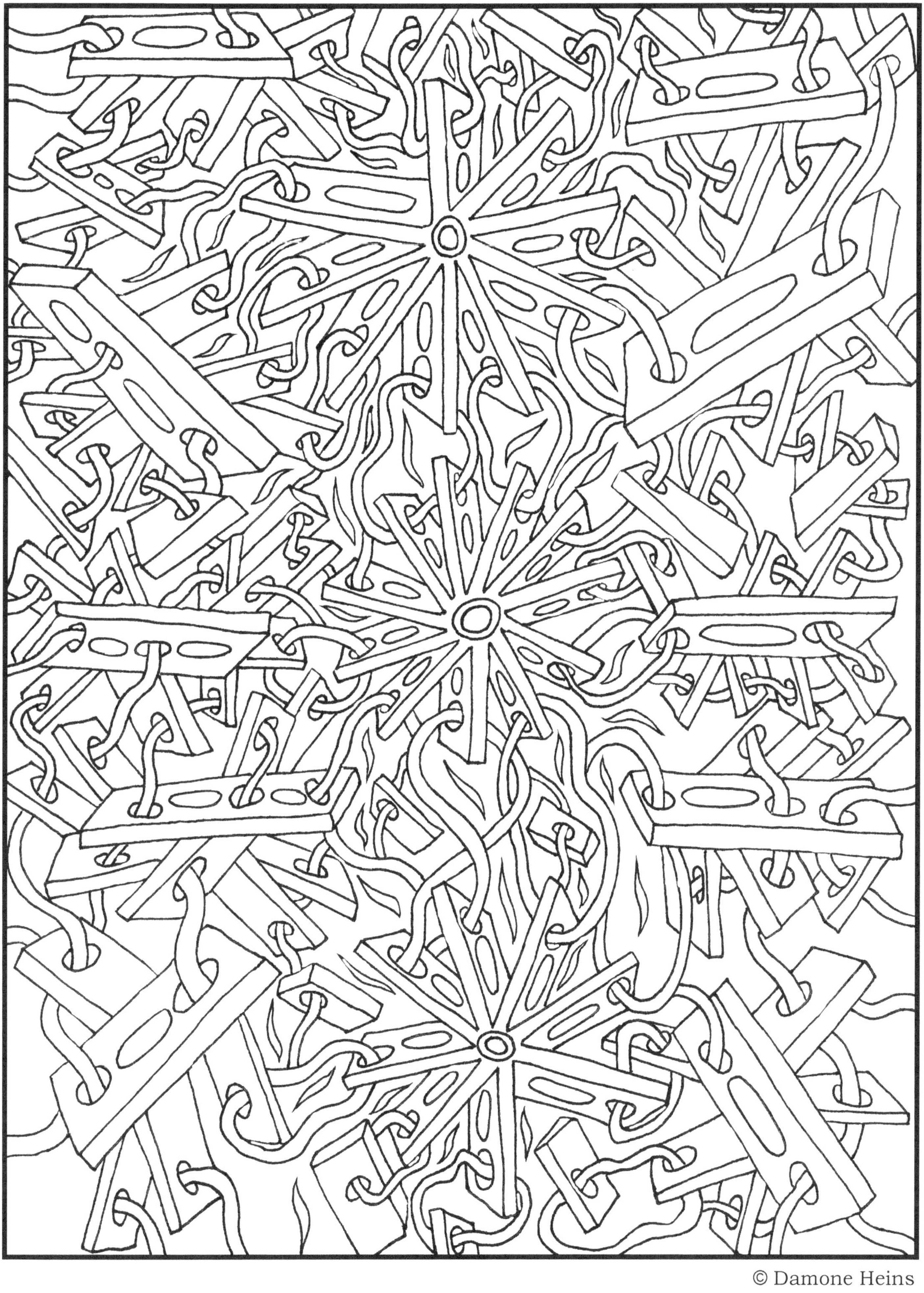

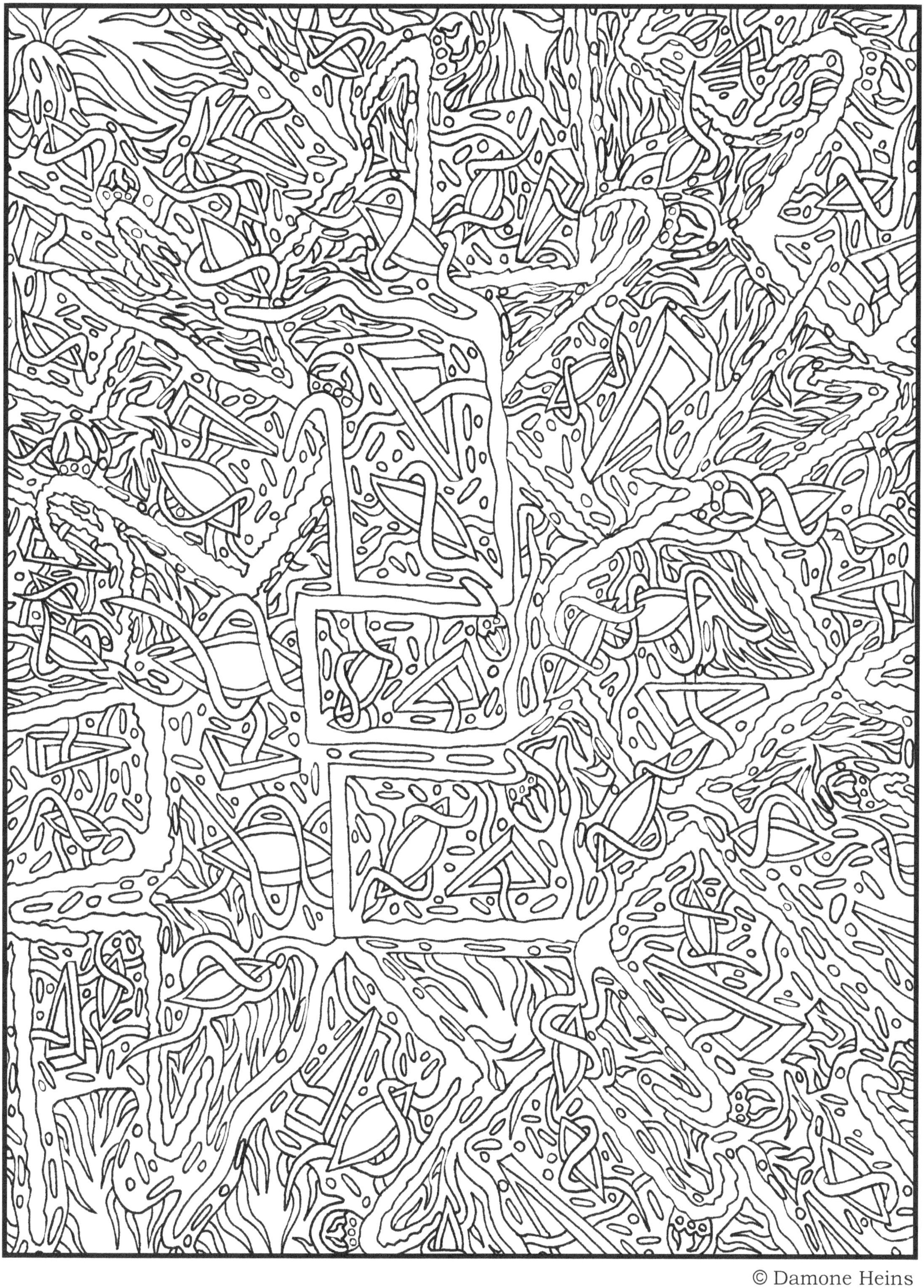

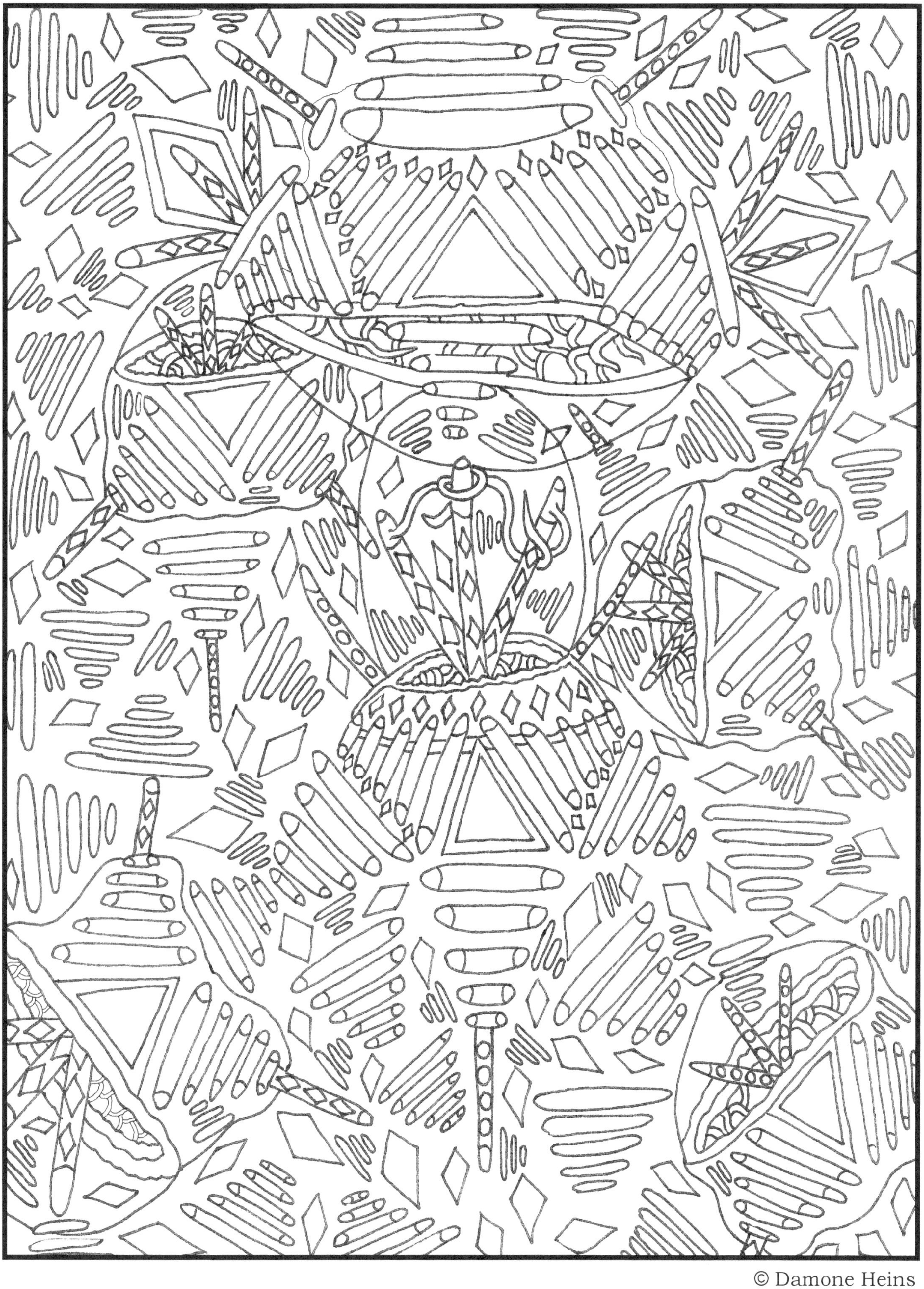

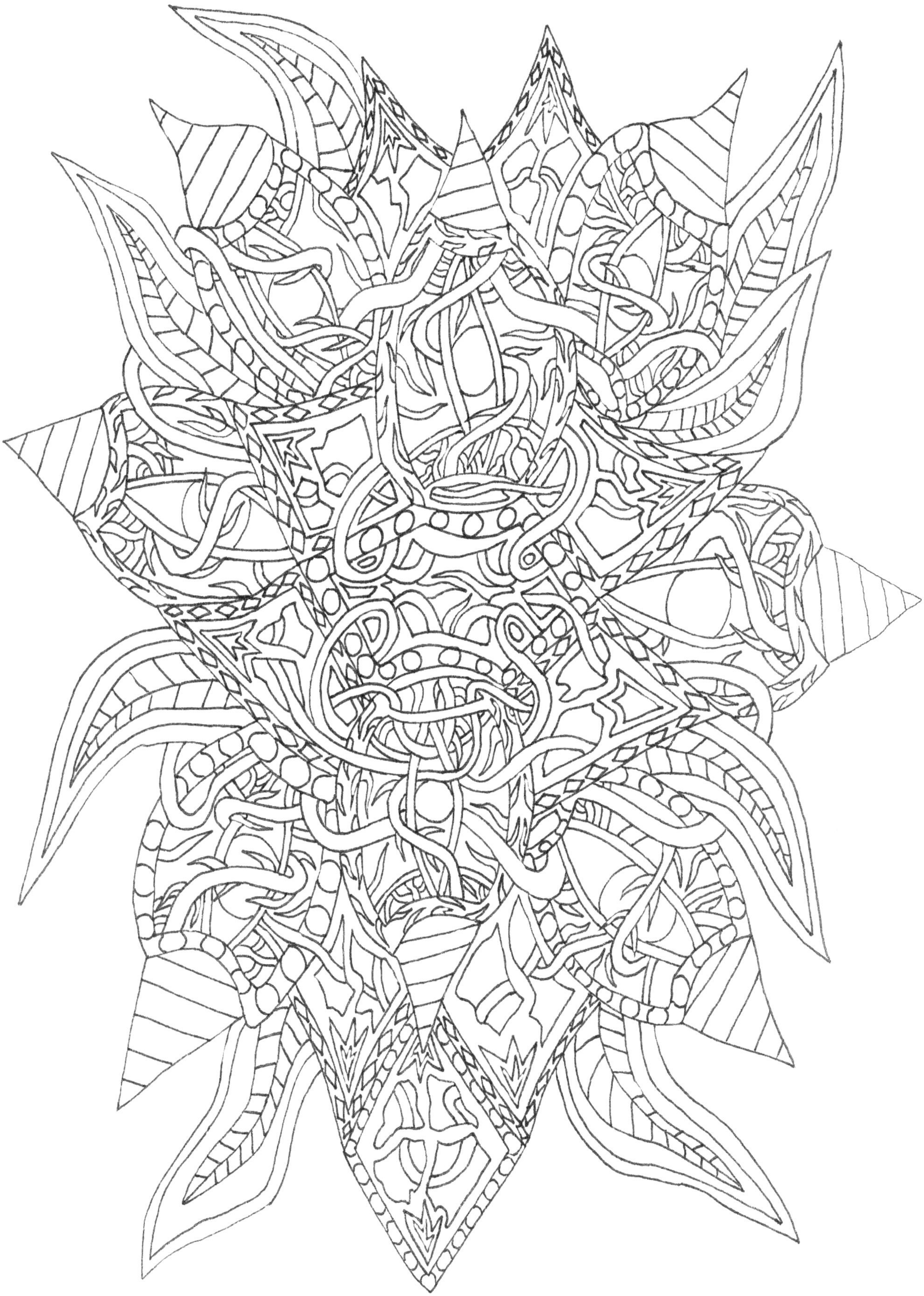

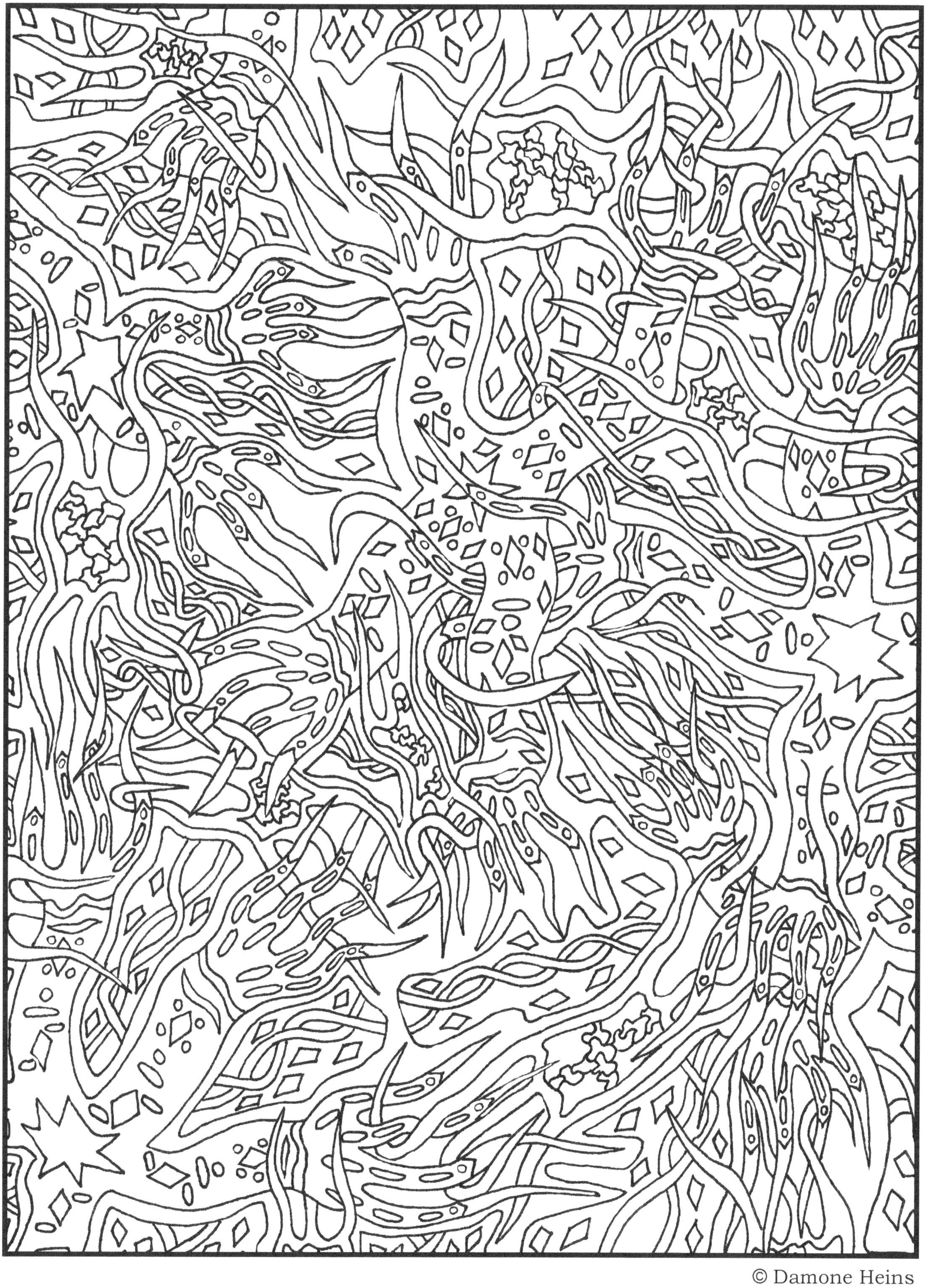

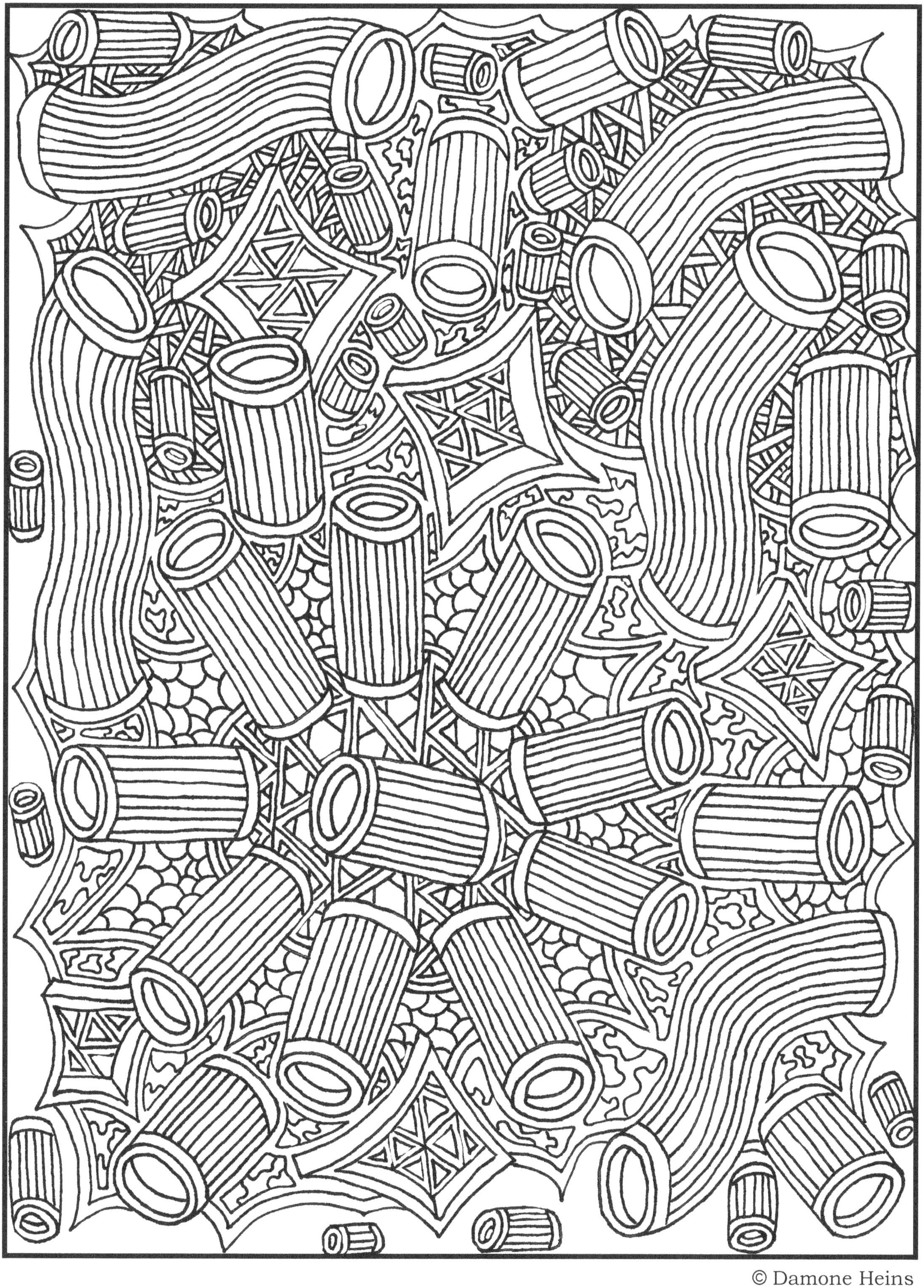

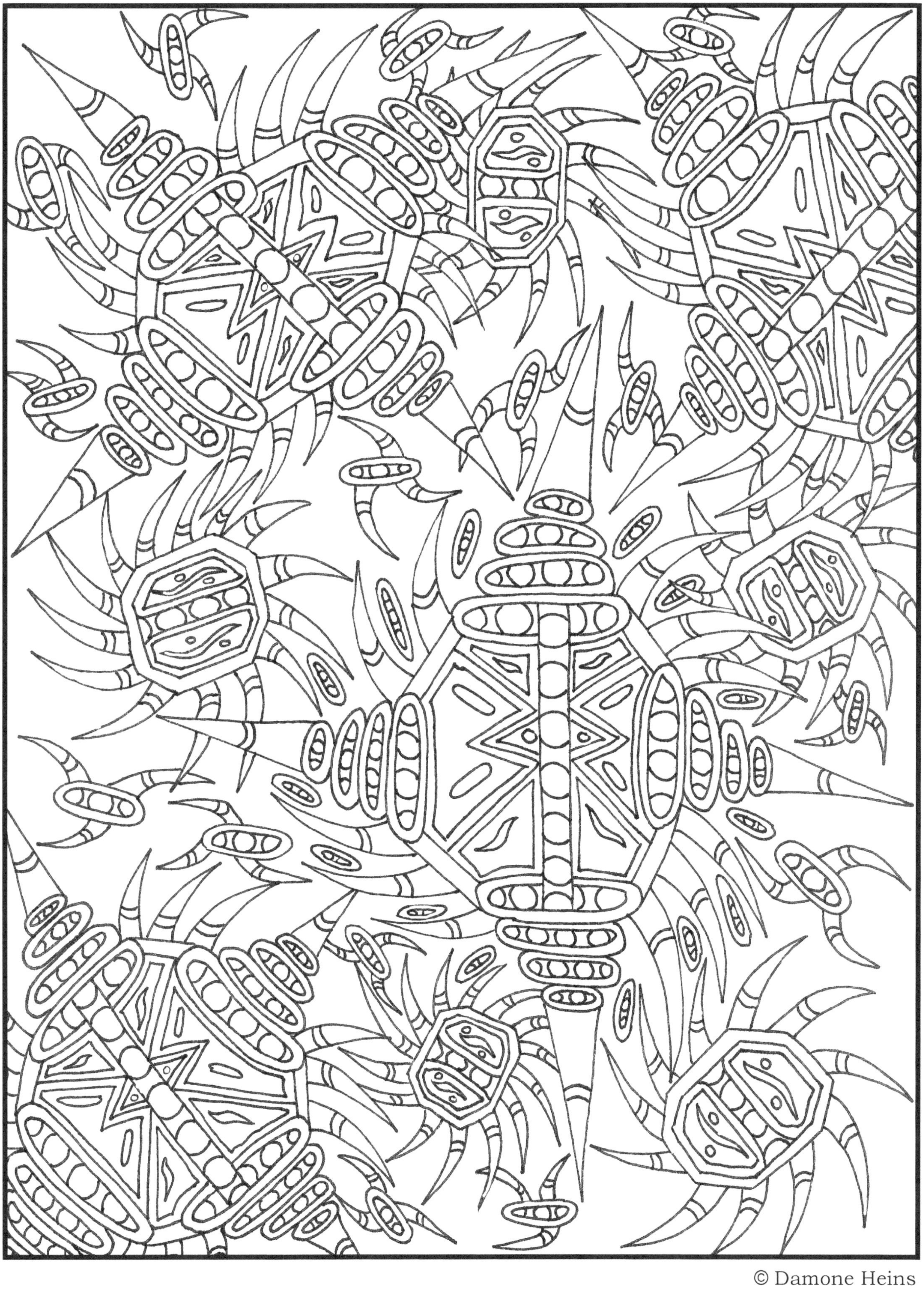

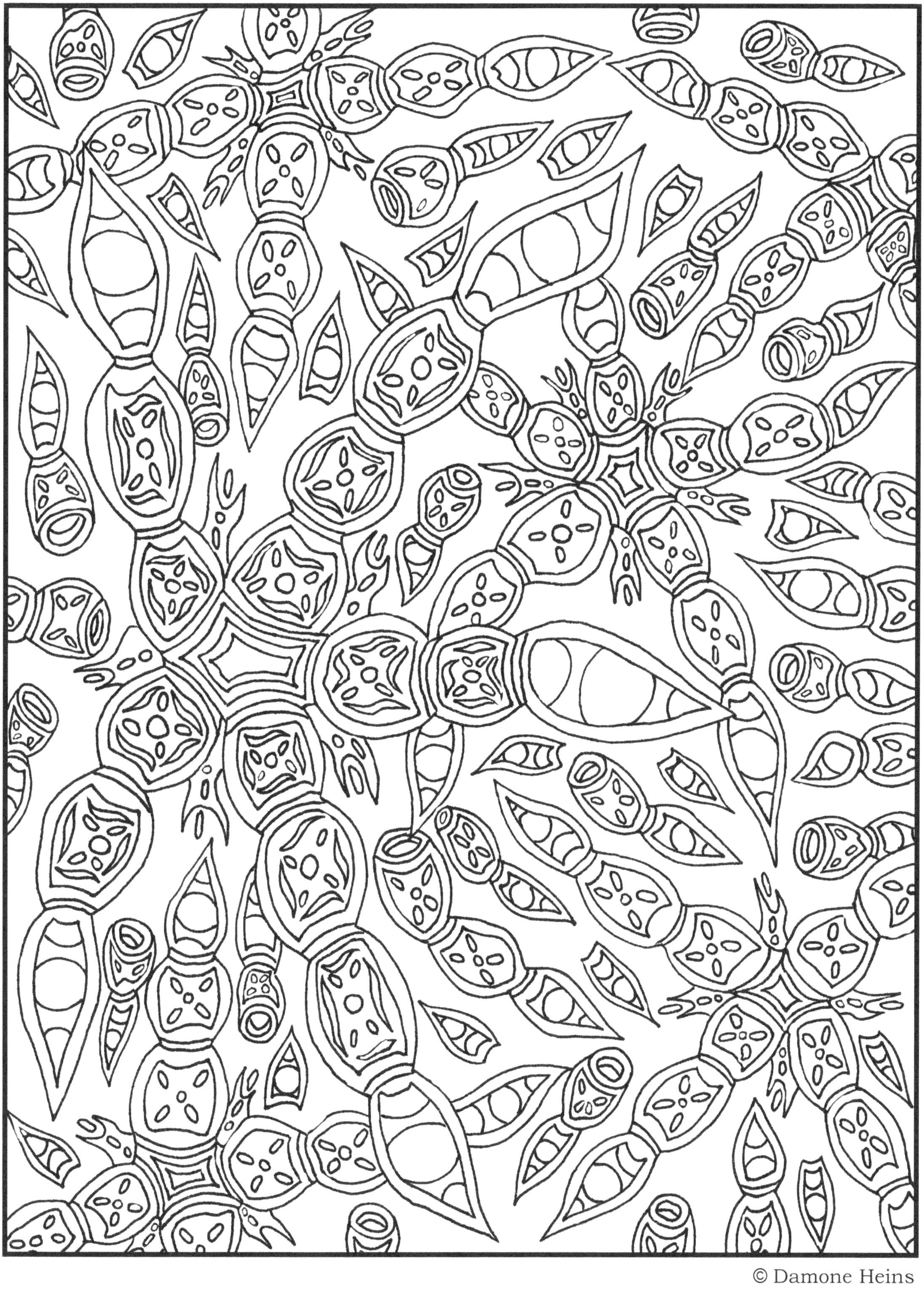

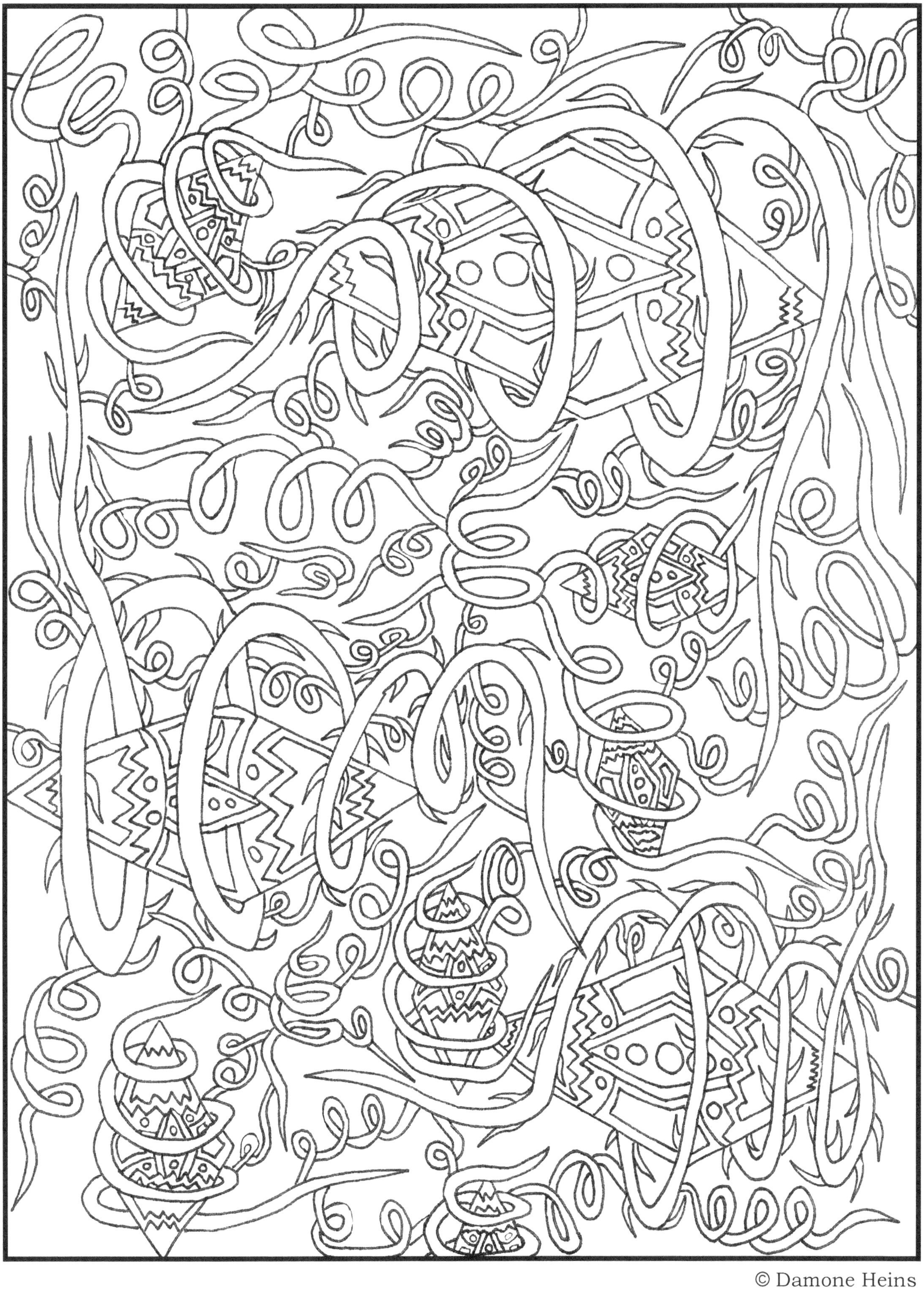

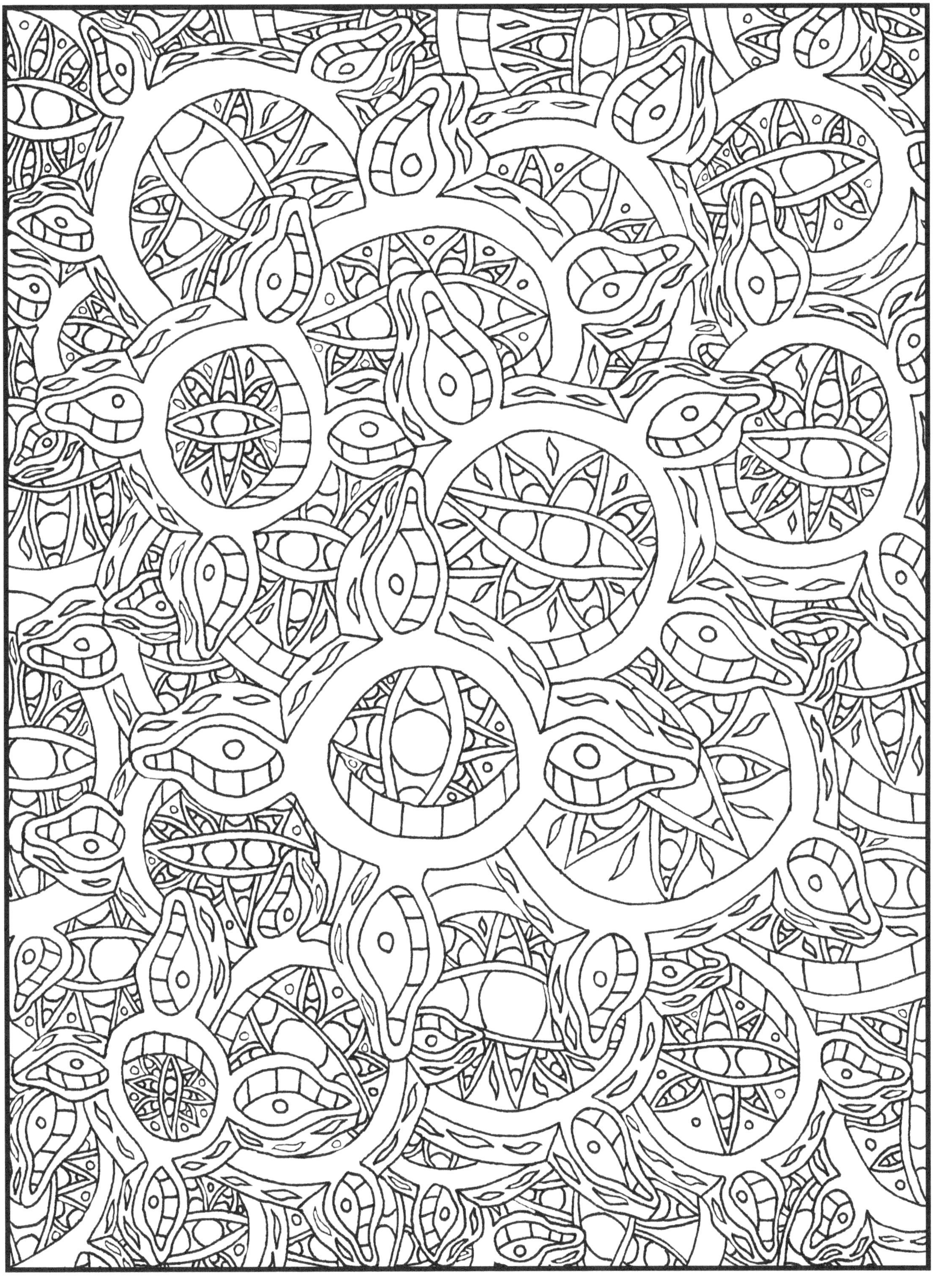

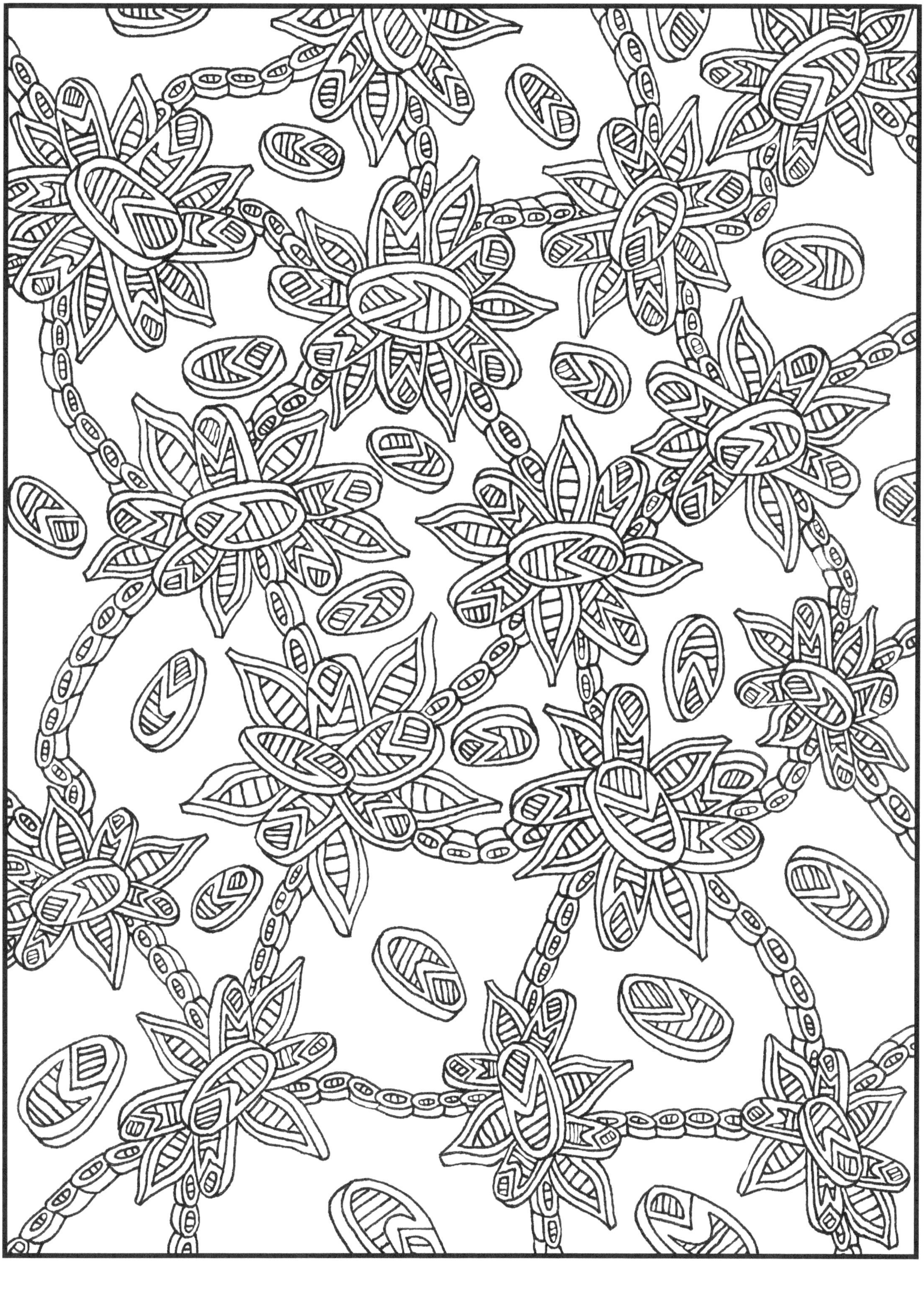

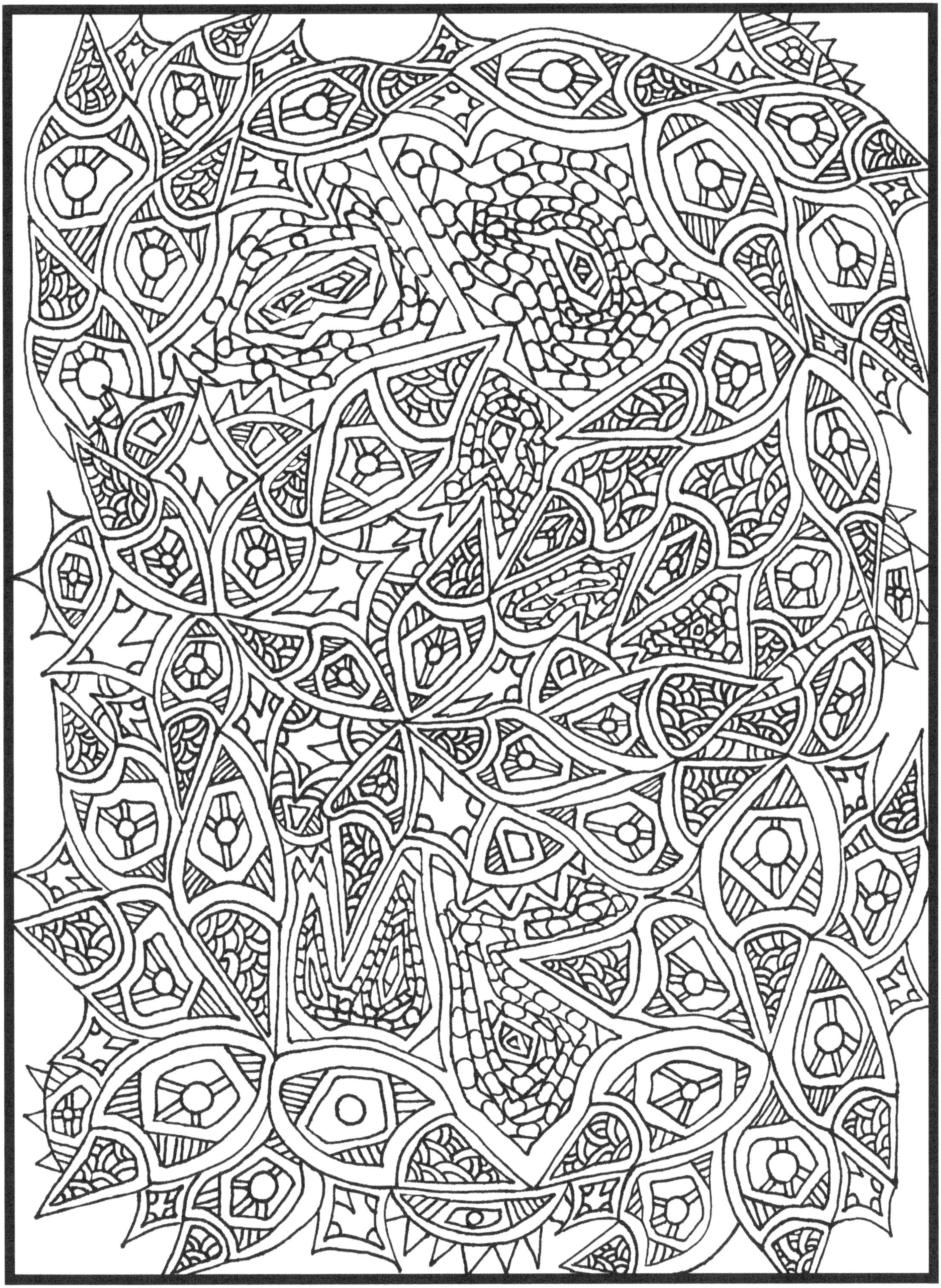

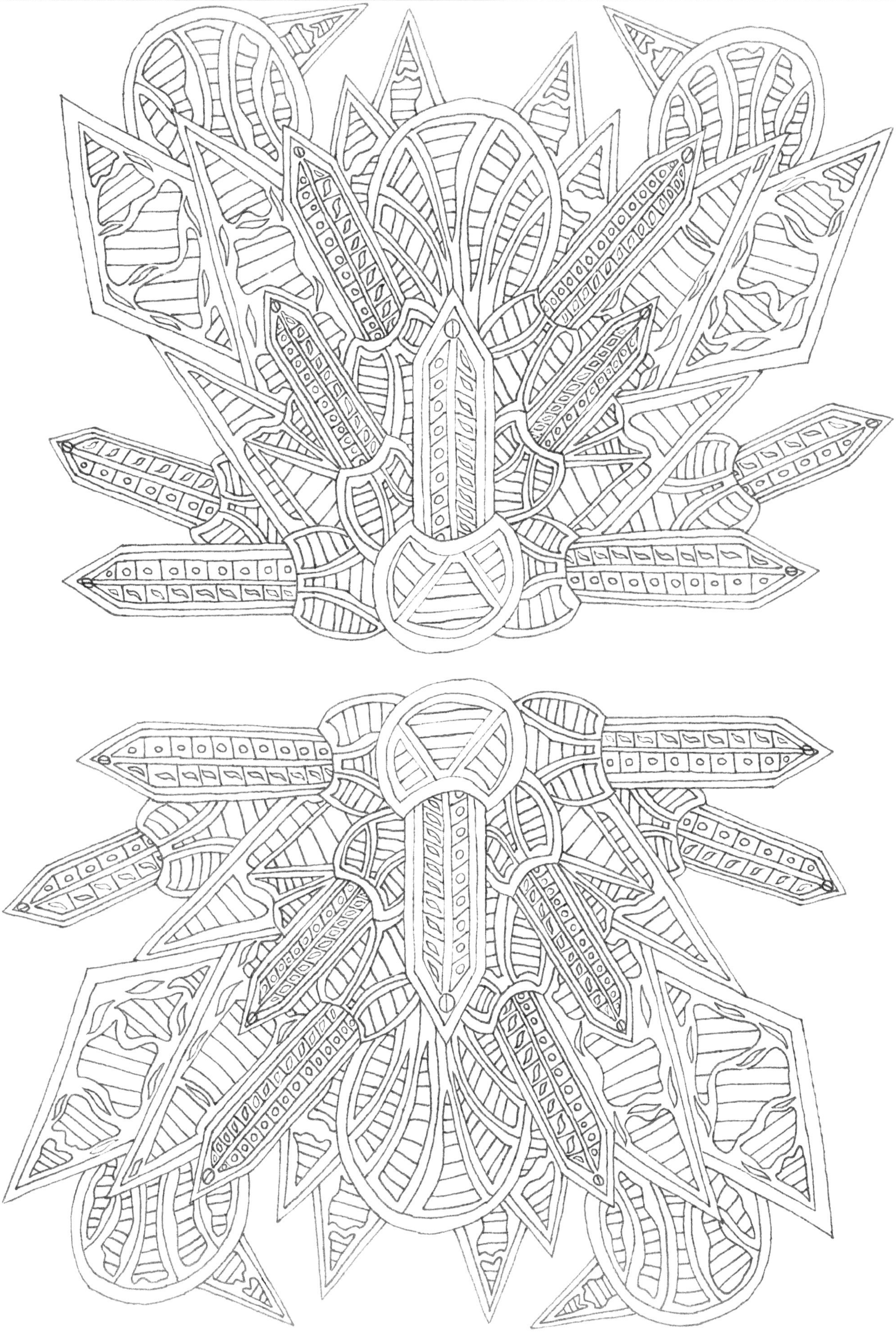

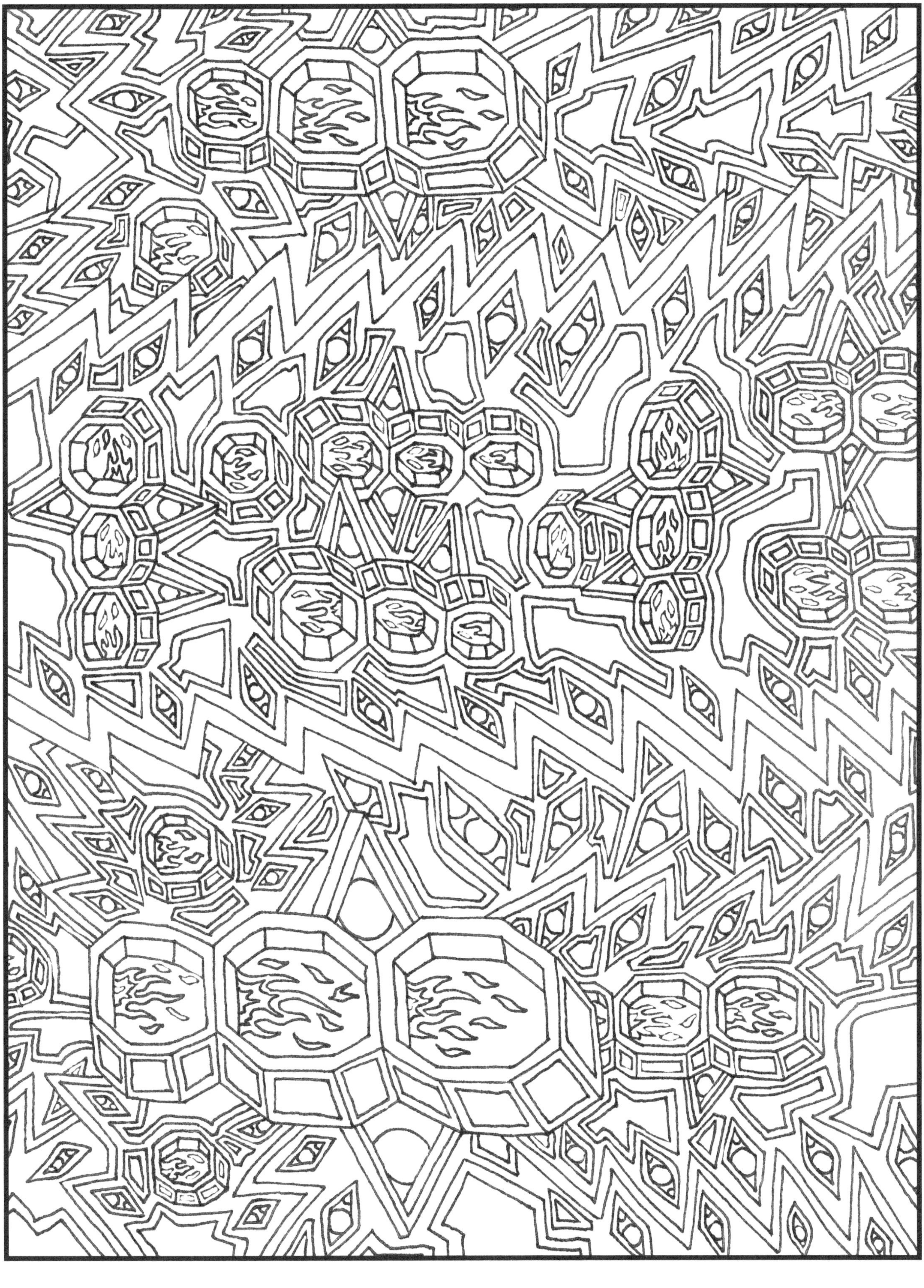

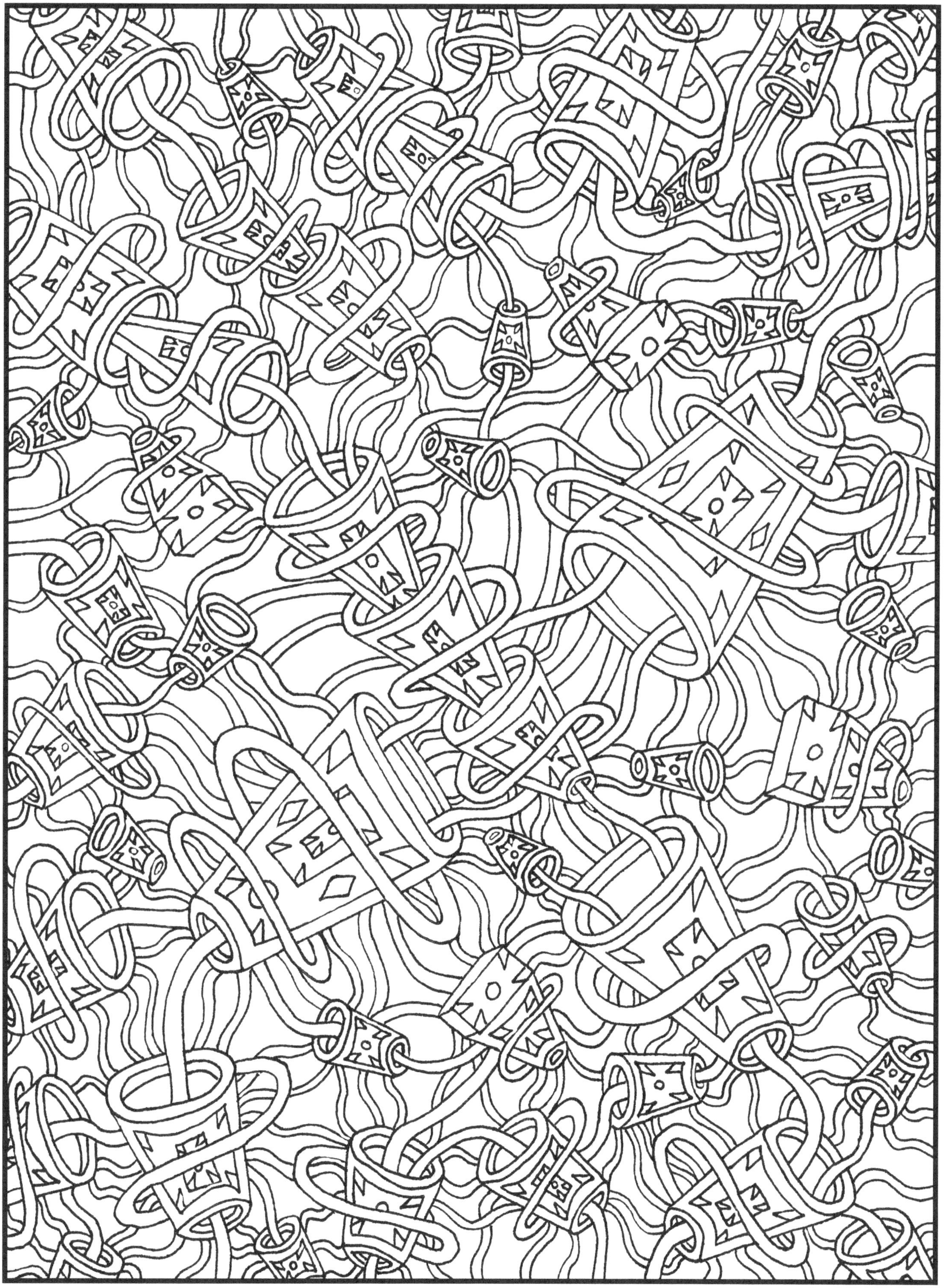

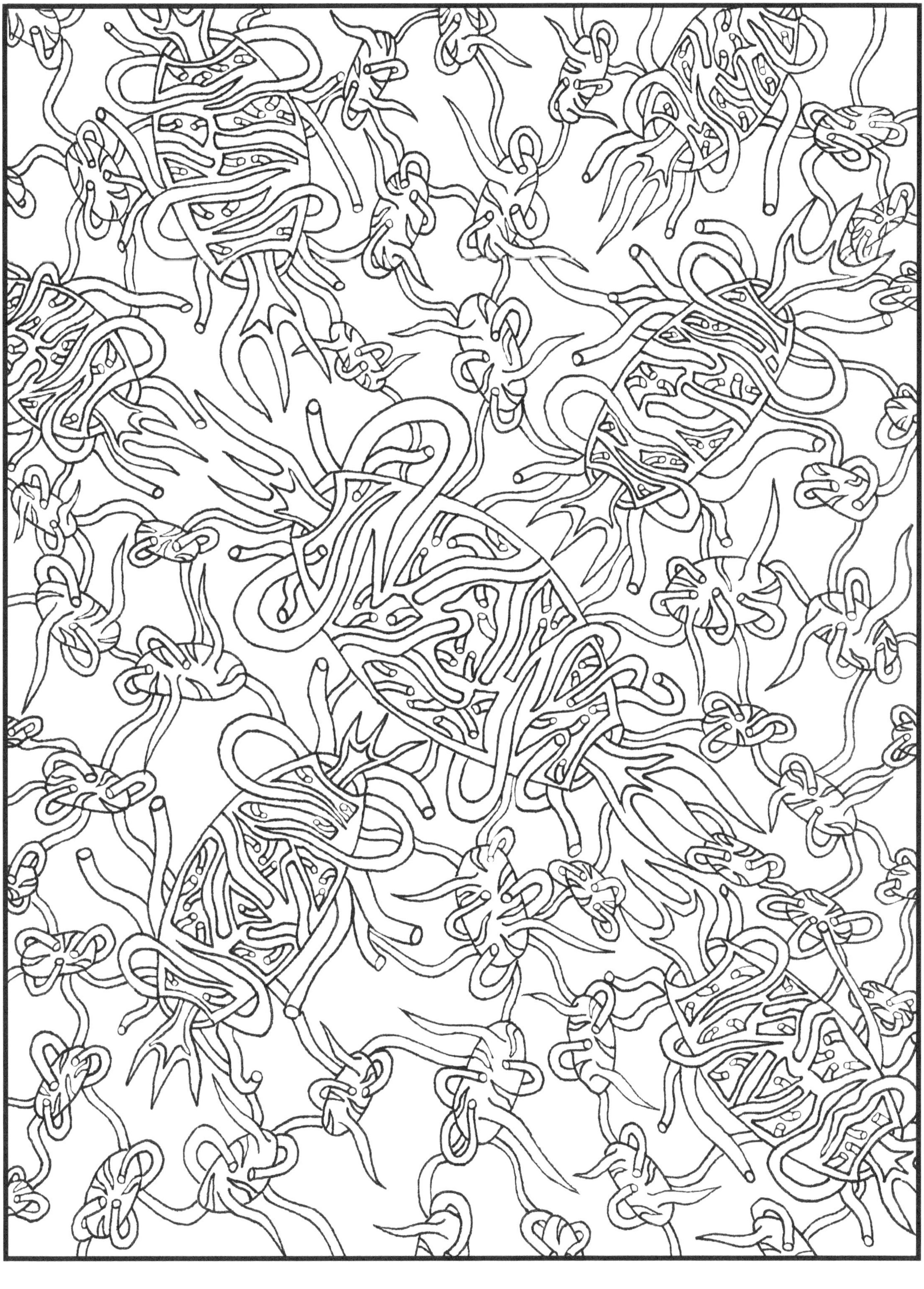

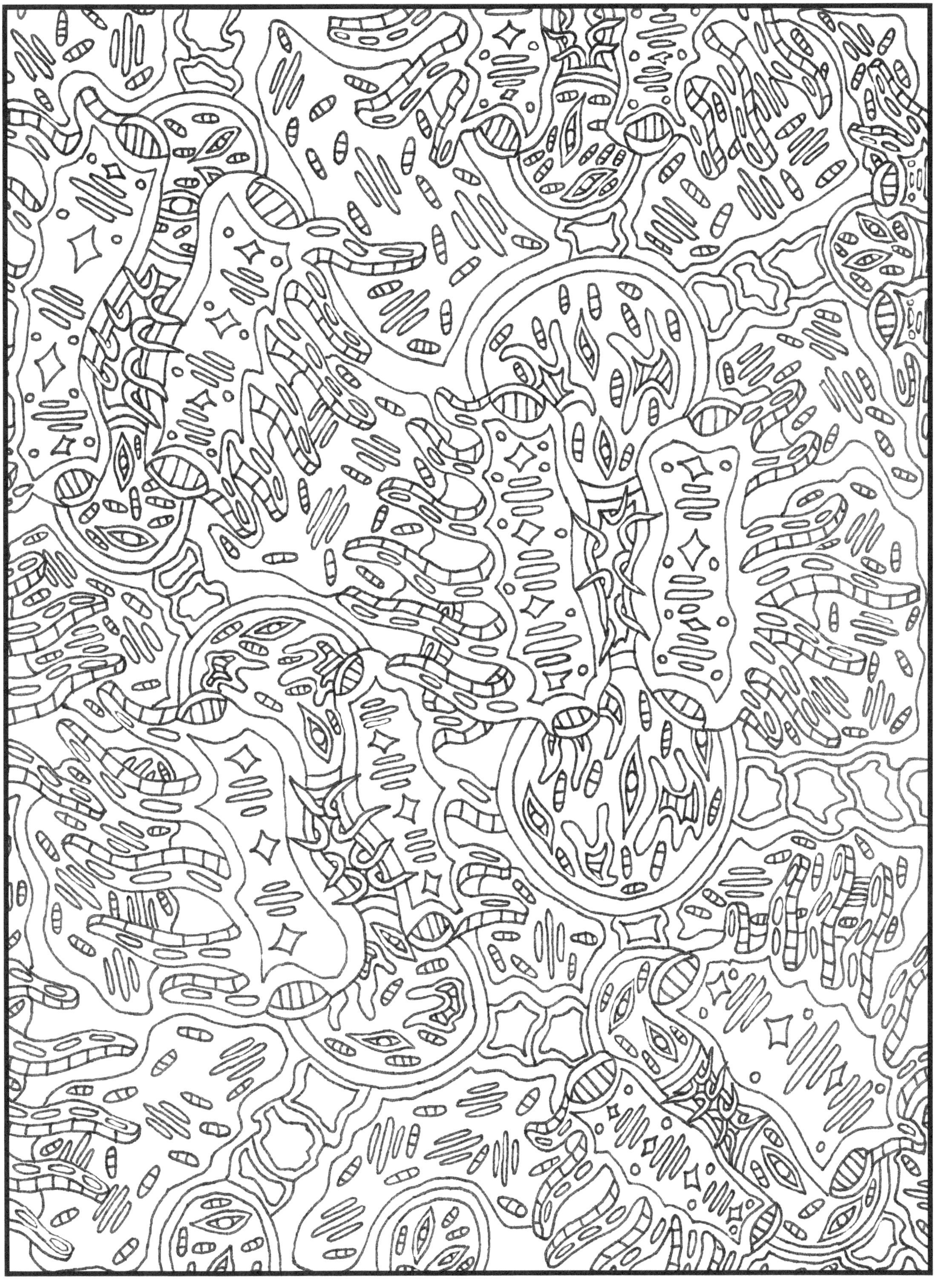

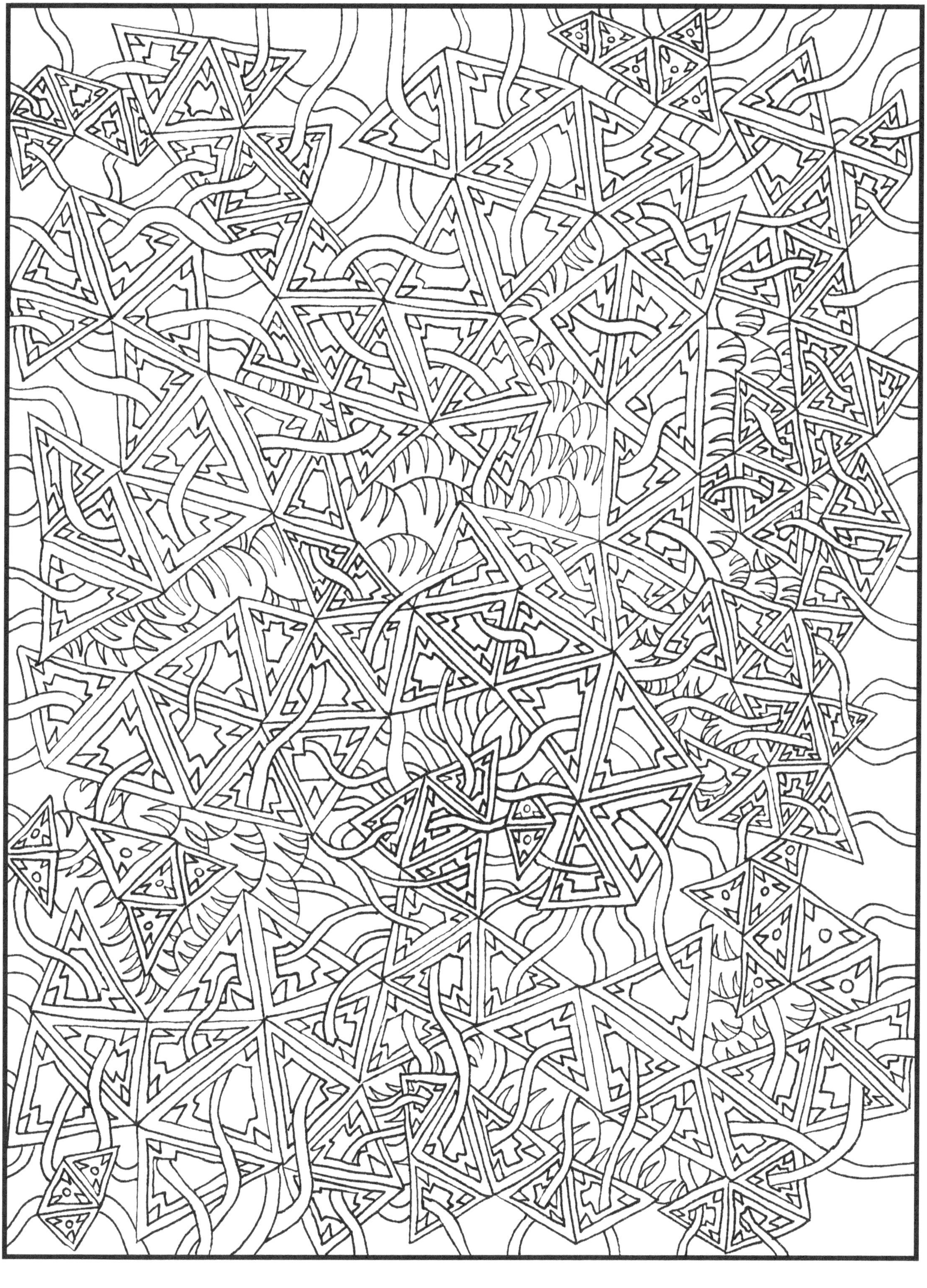

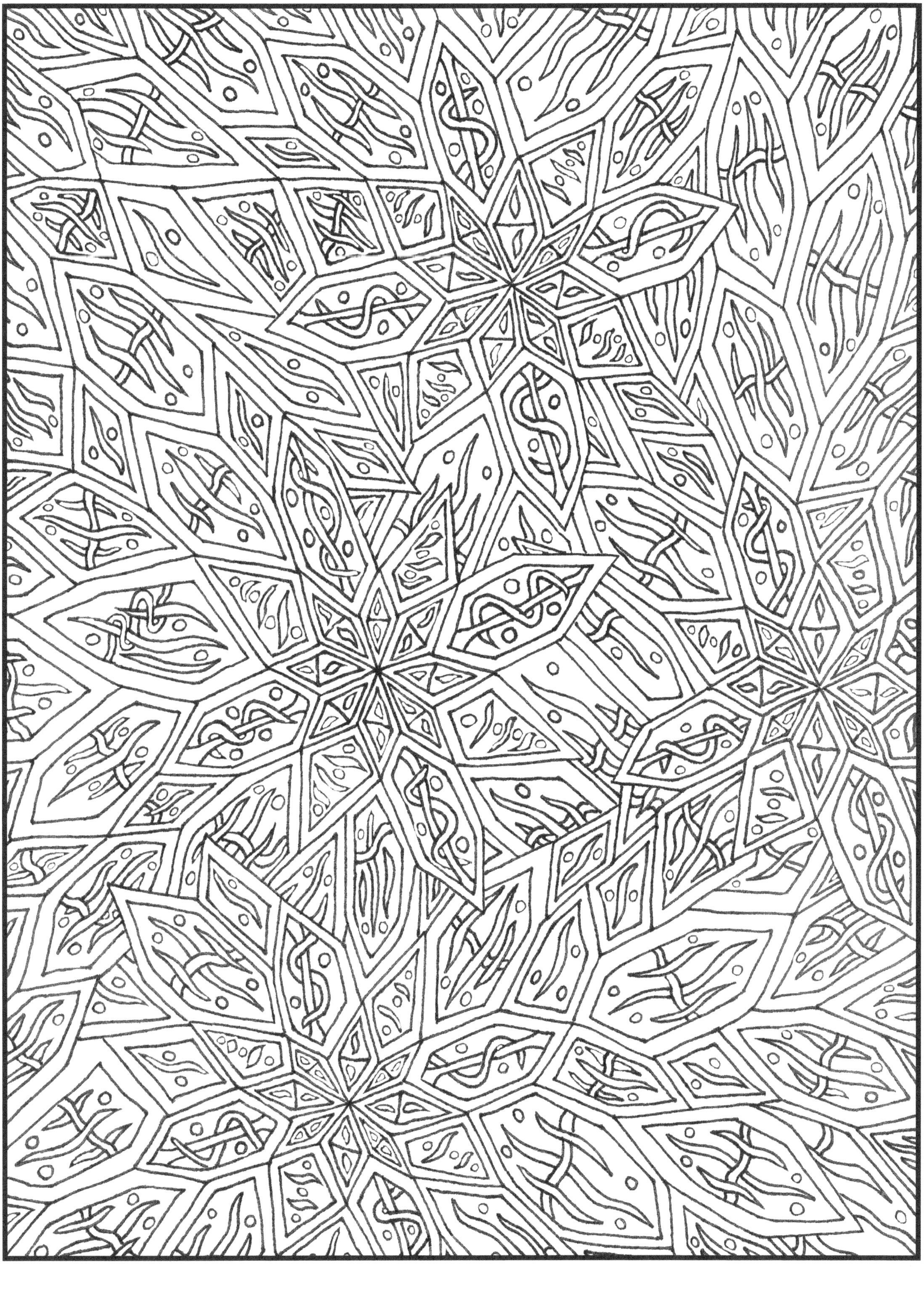

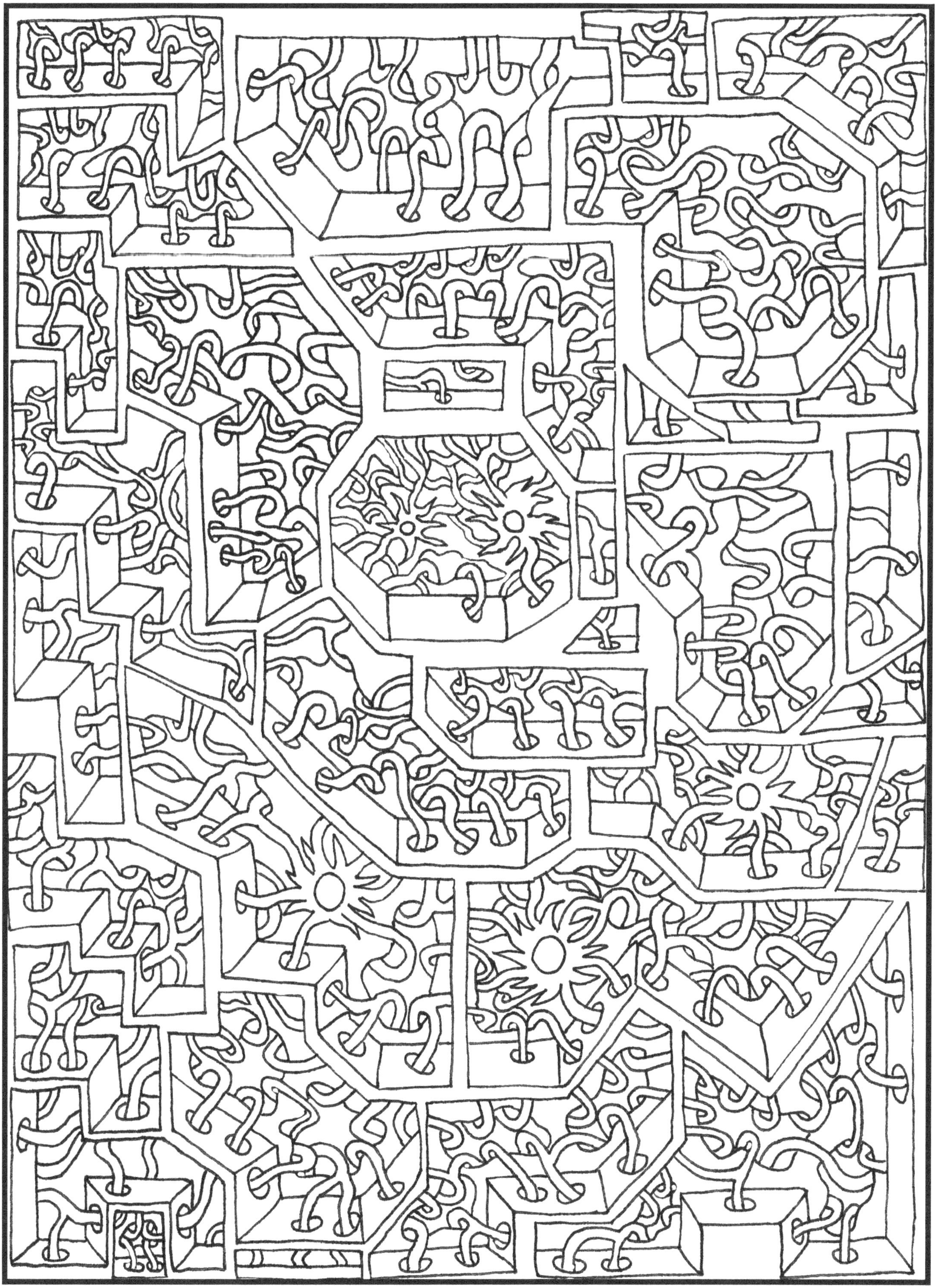

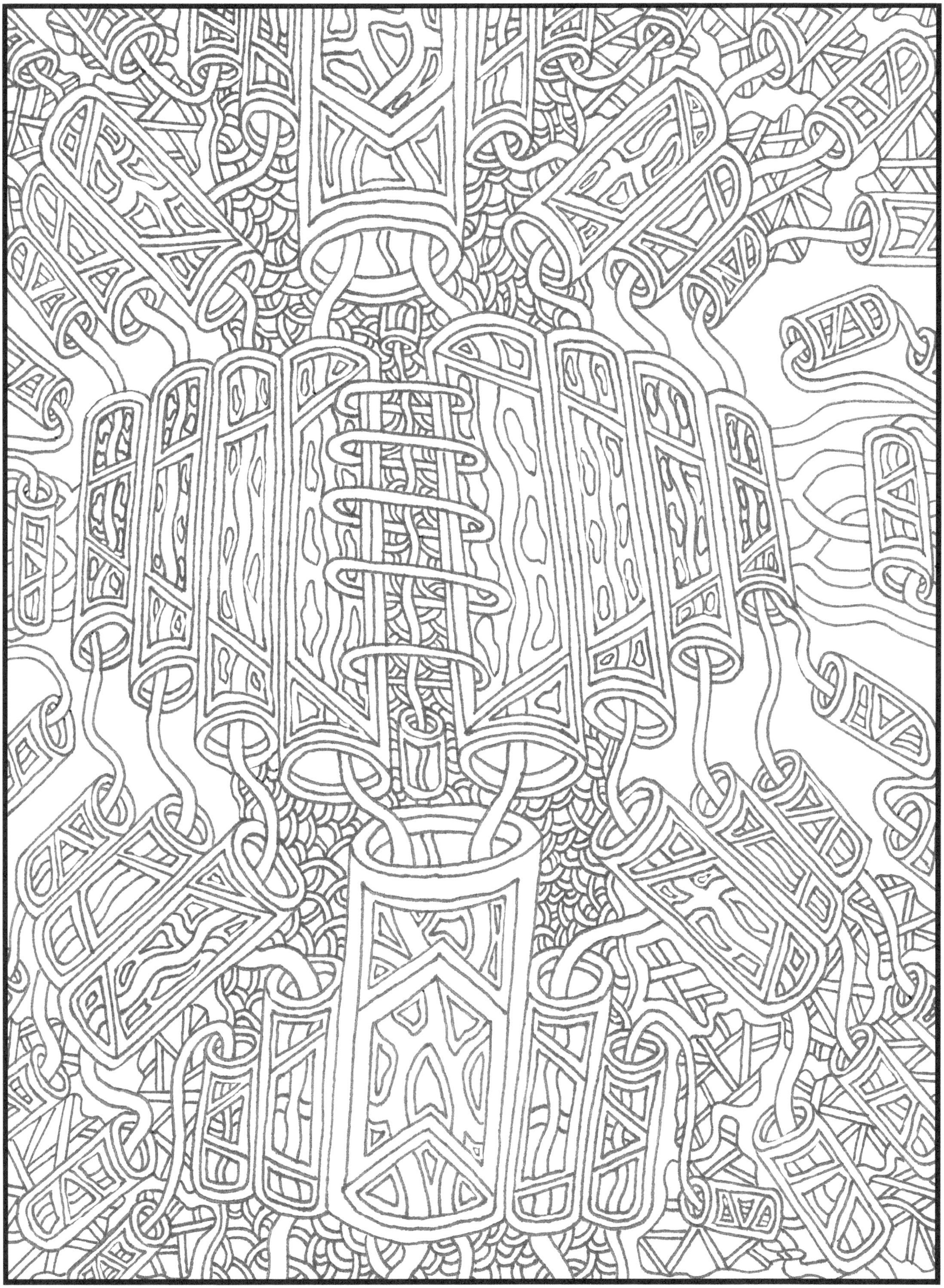

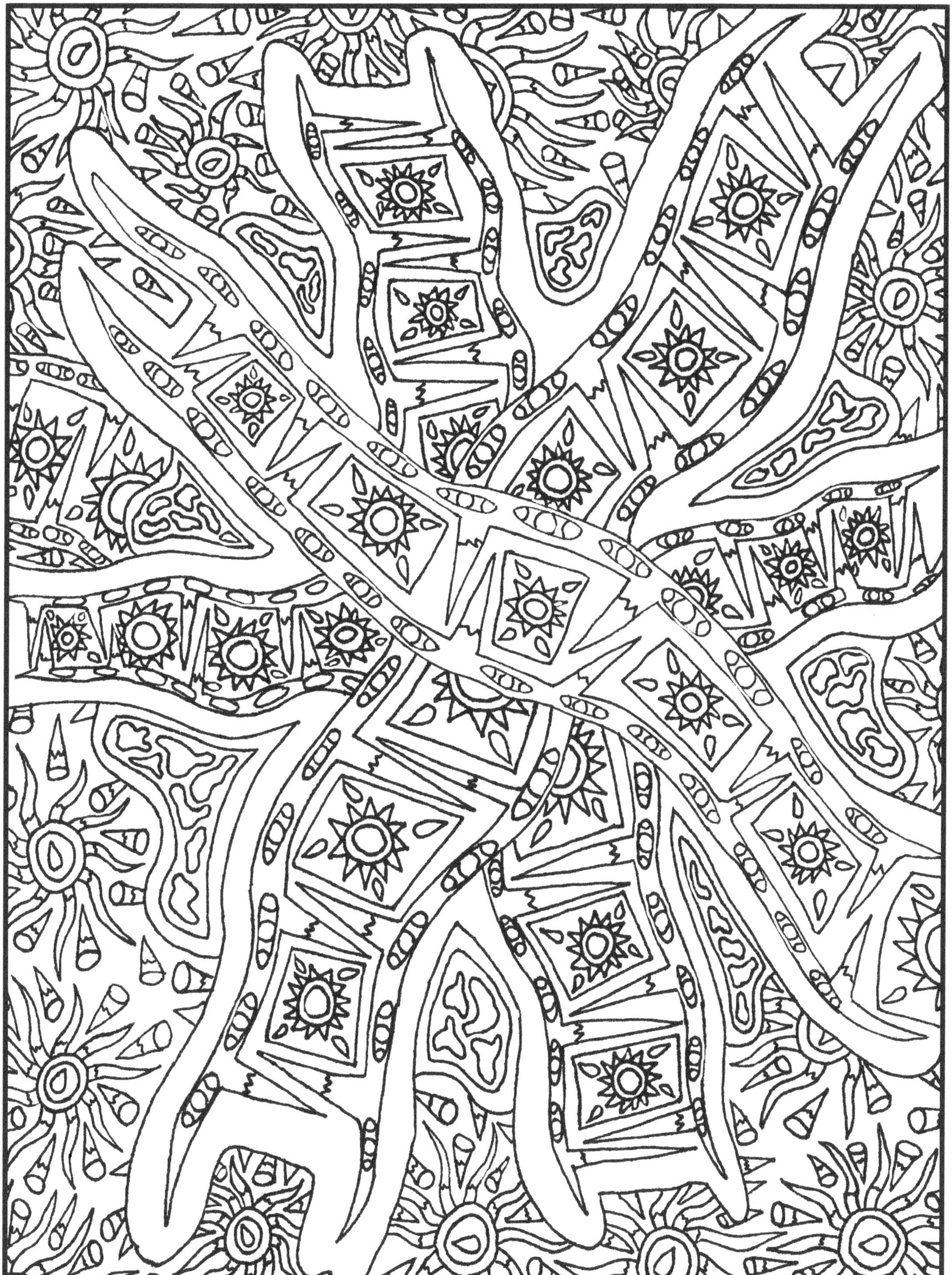

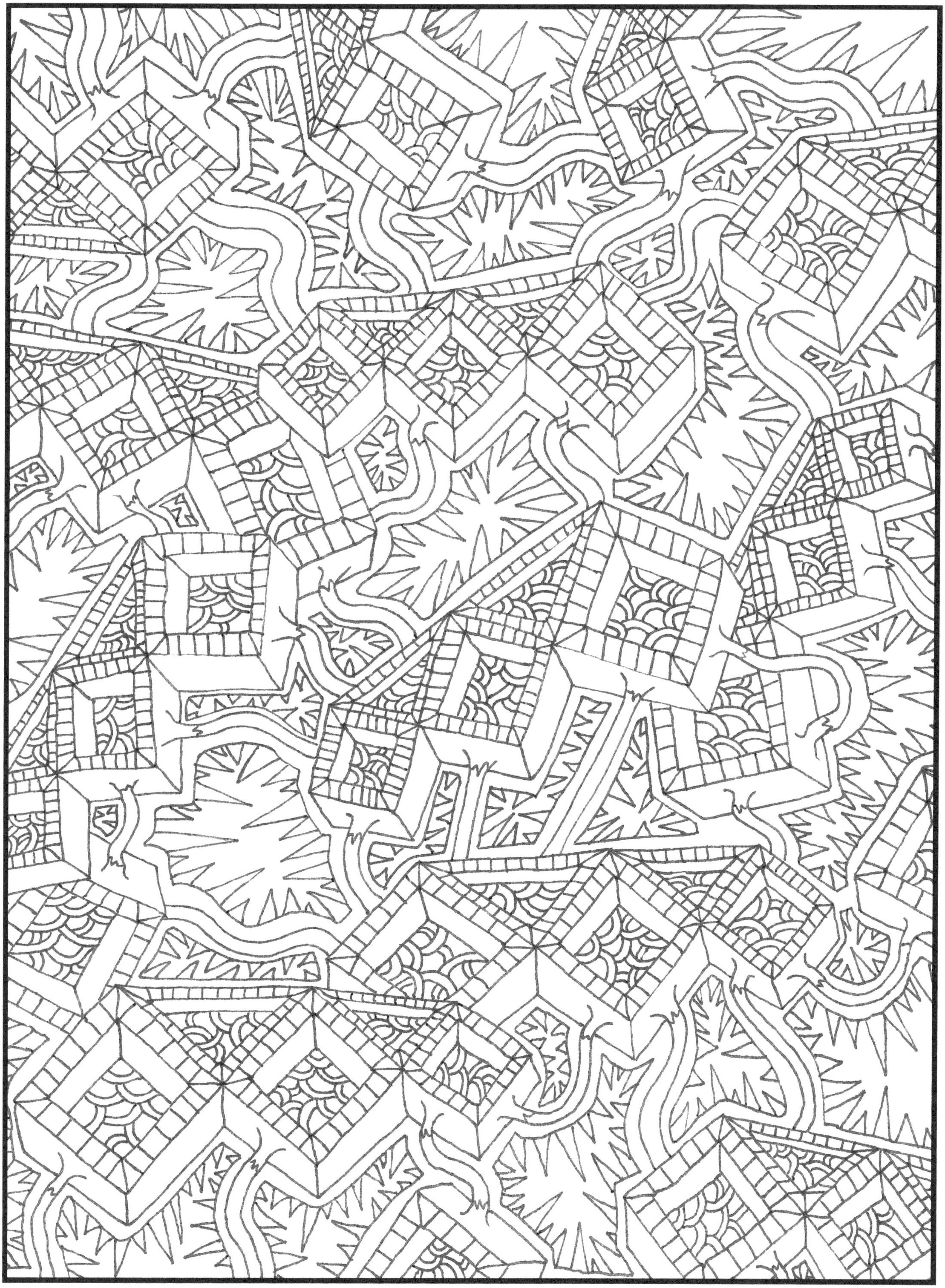

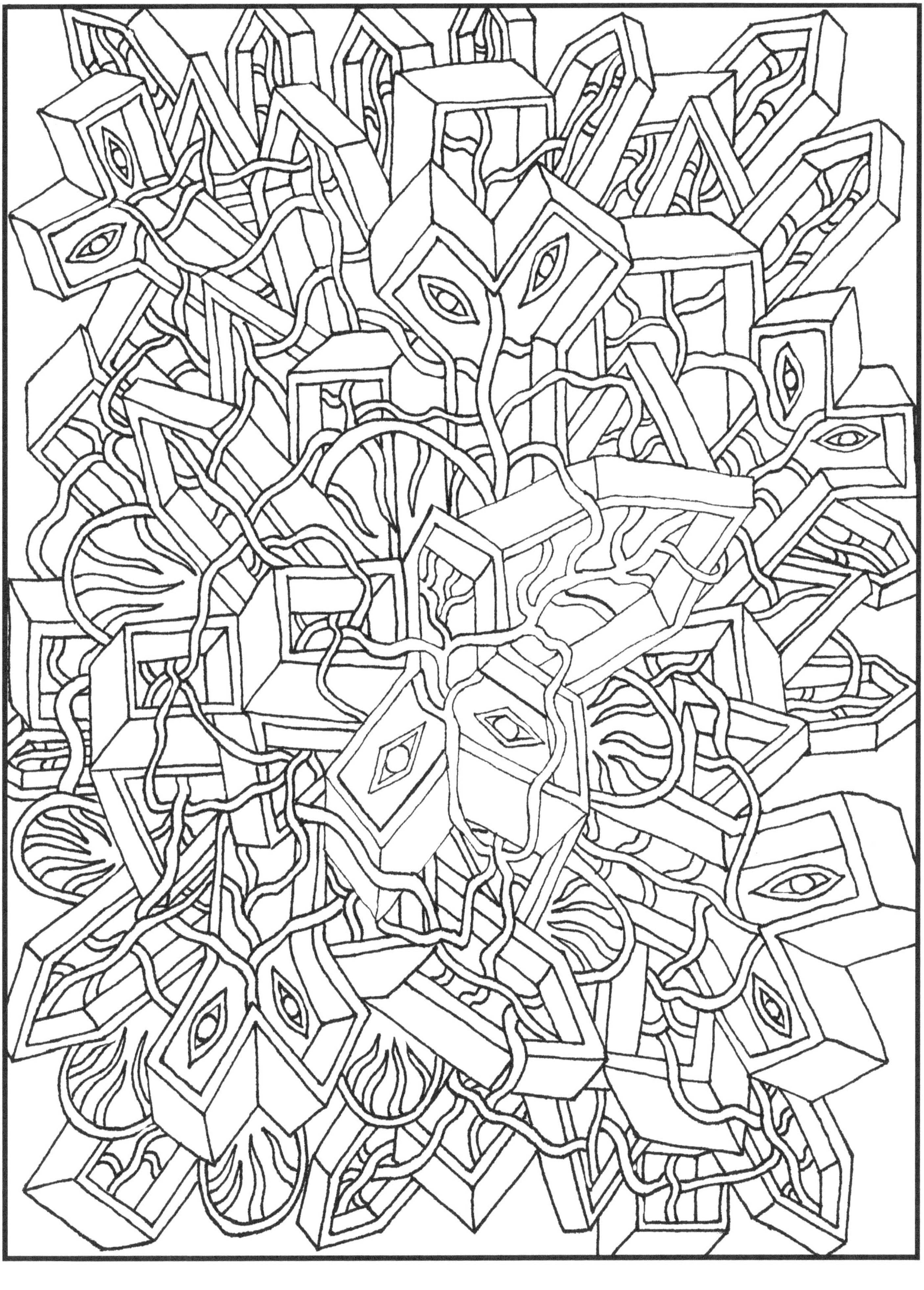

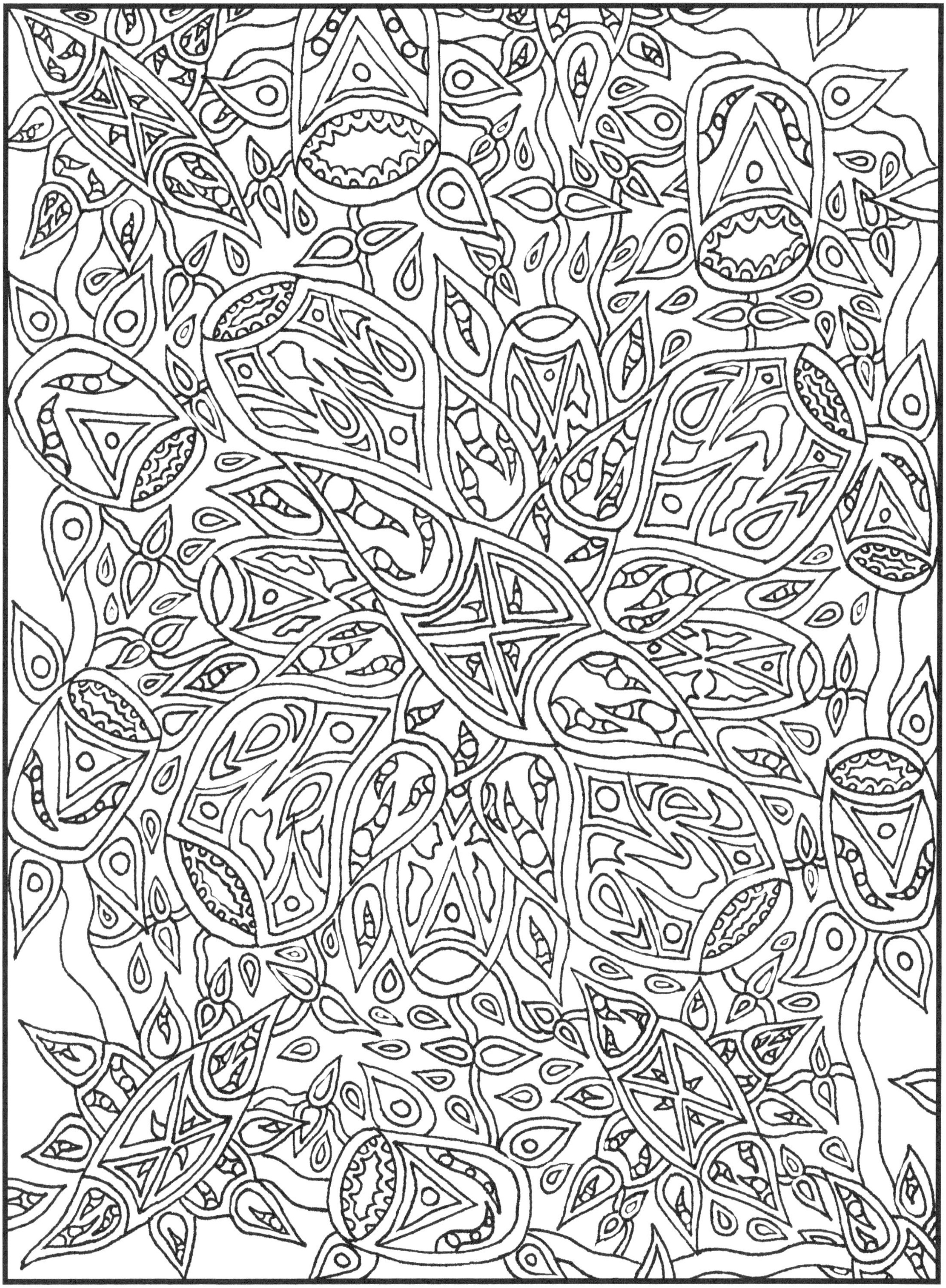

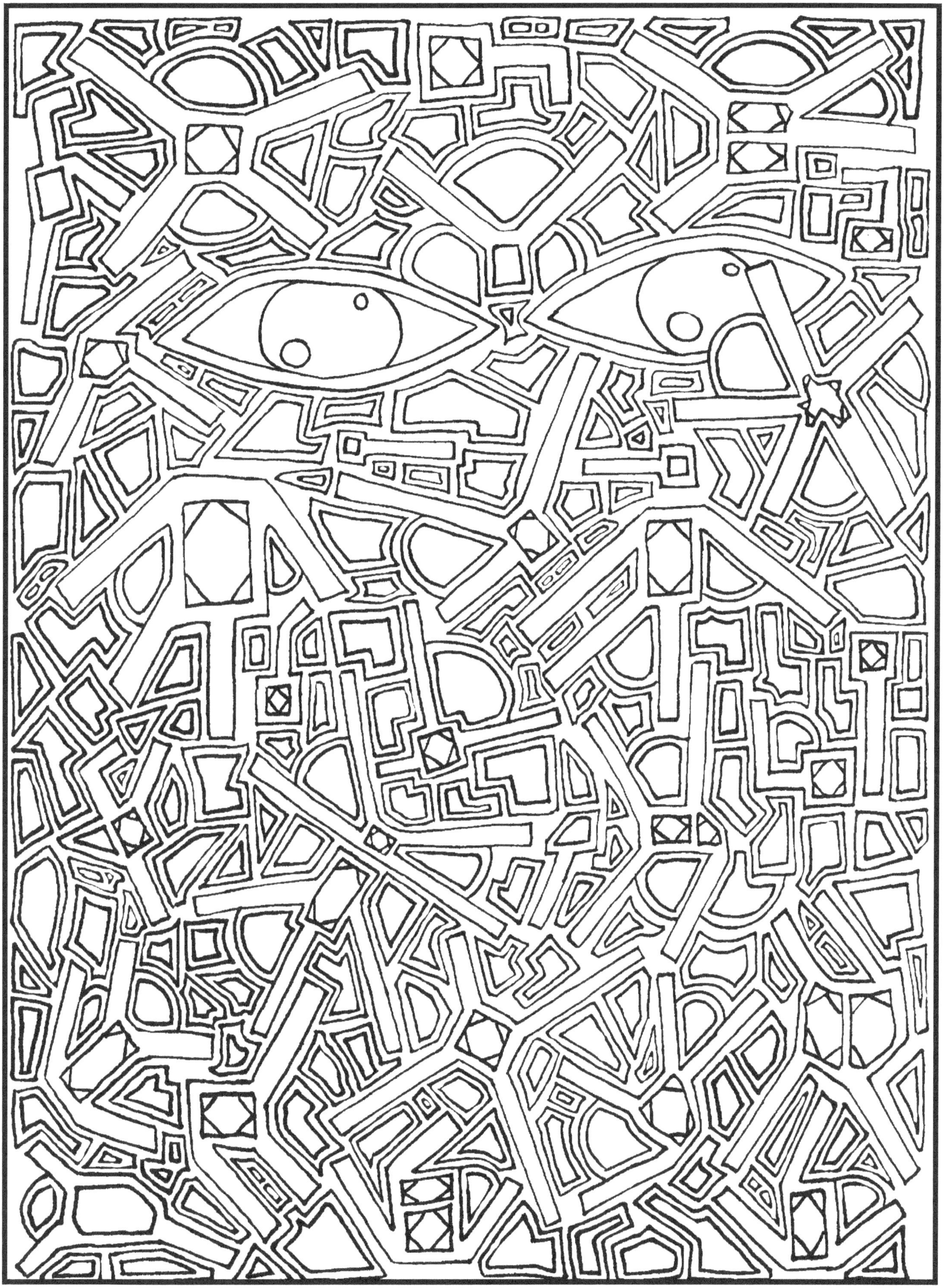

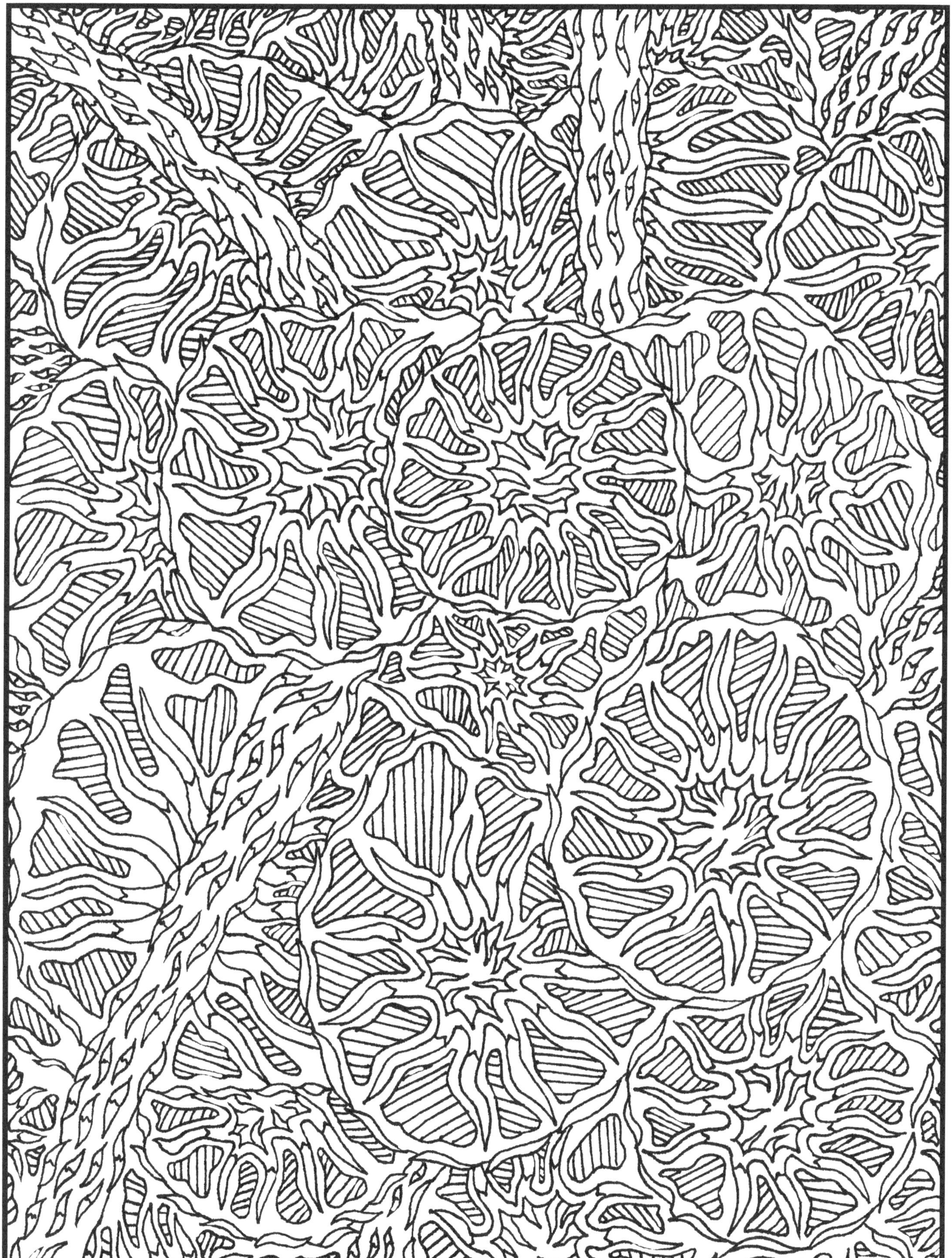

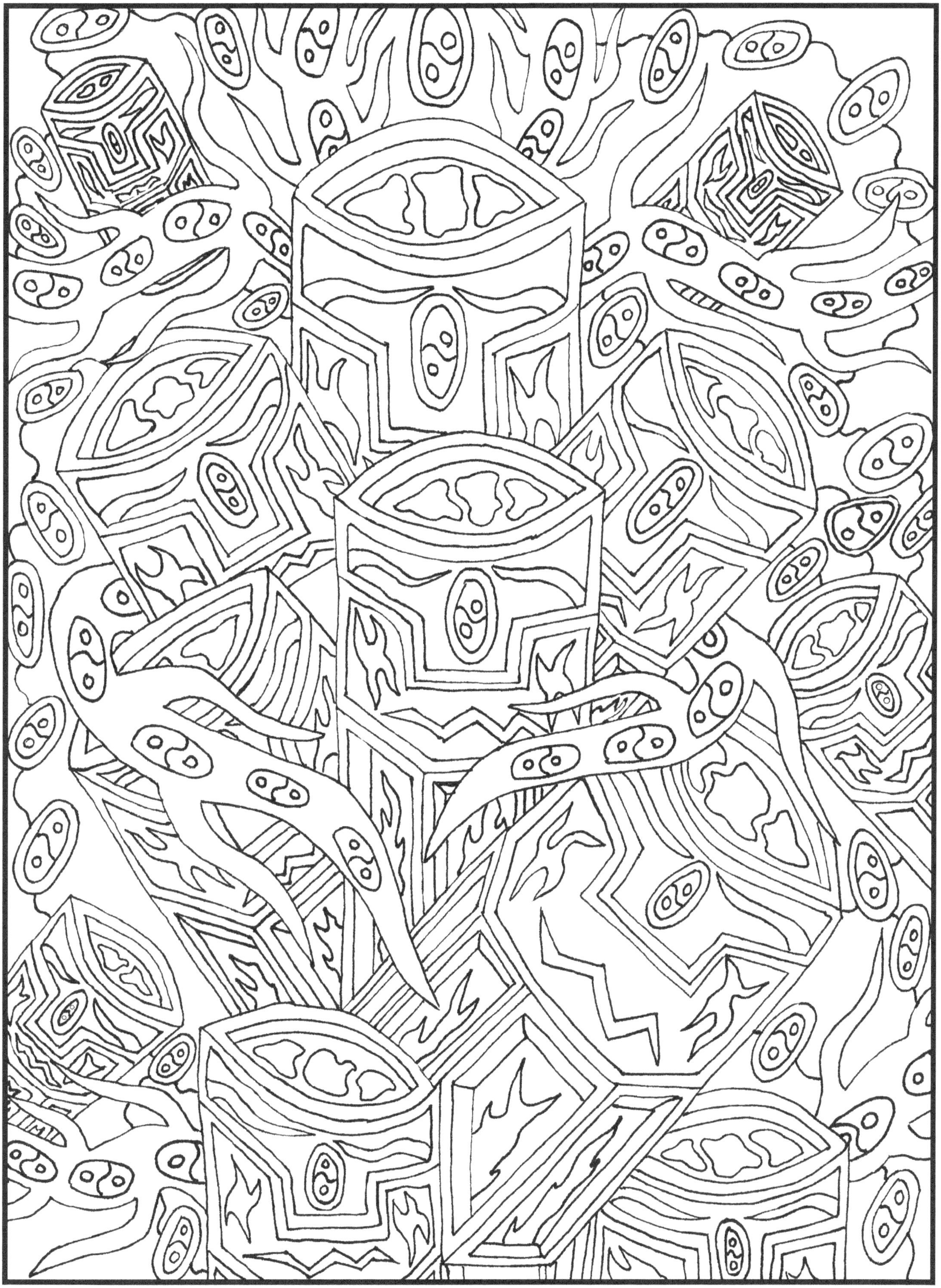

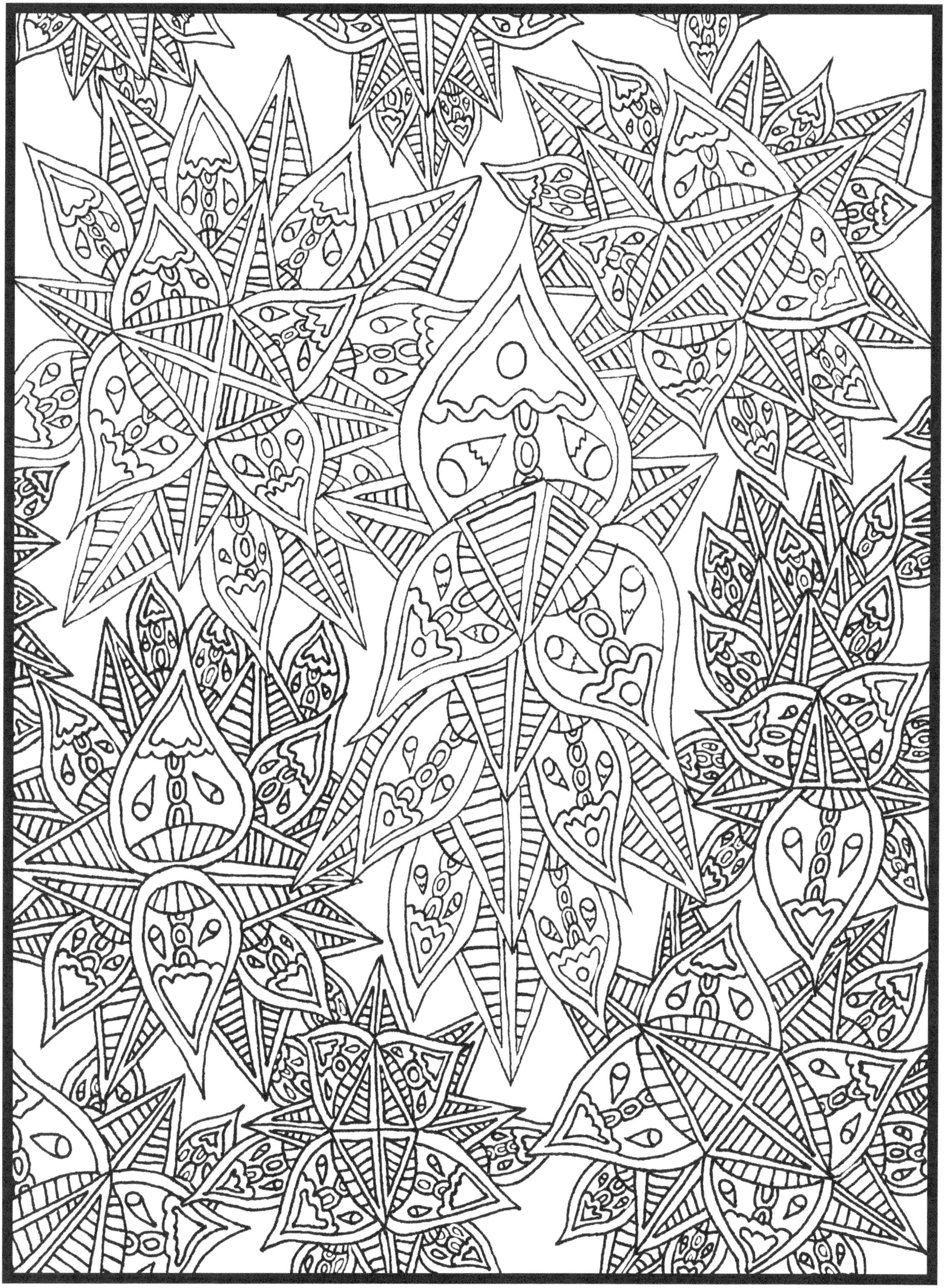

For more books
email me at damonehe@yahoo.com
or mail me at PO. box
2433 Newport Oregon
97365
or you can visit damonesart.com

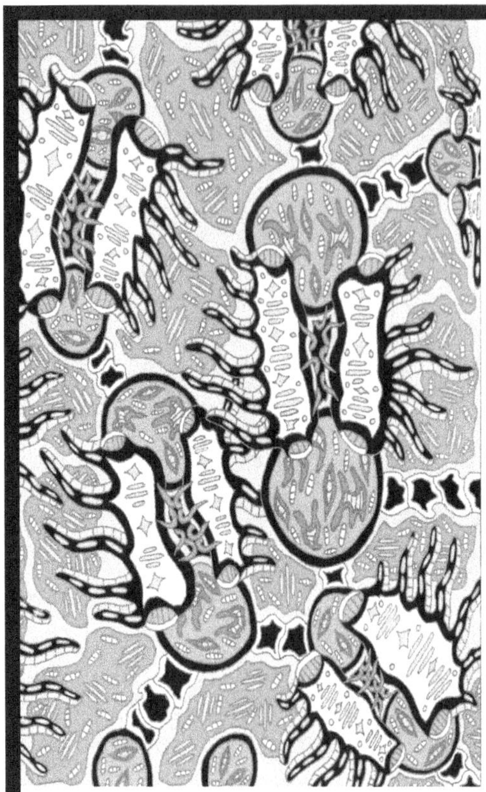
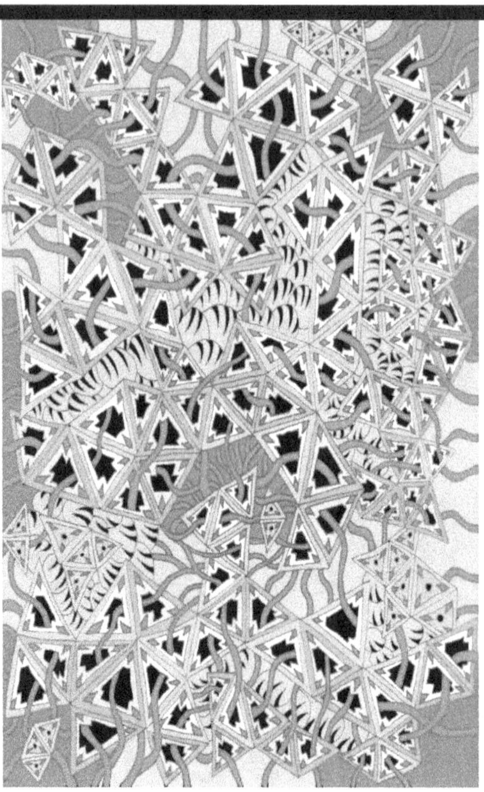
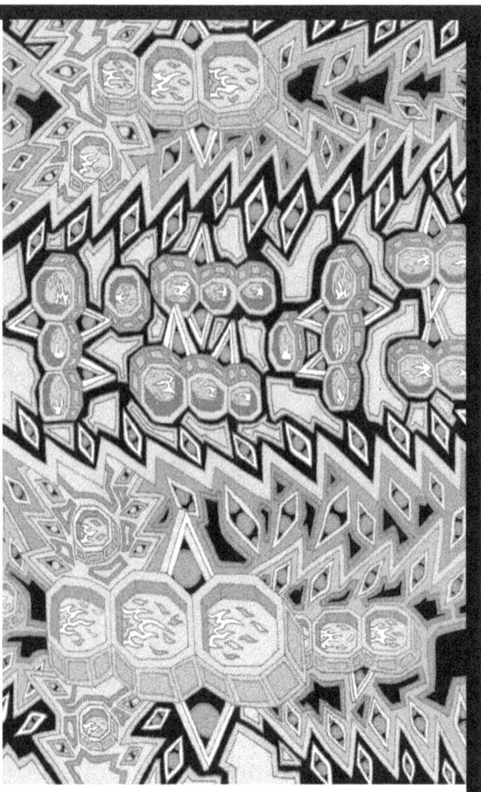

All Abstract Art Done By Damone Heins

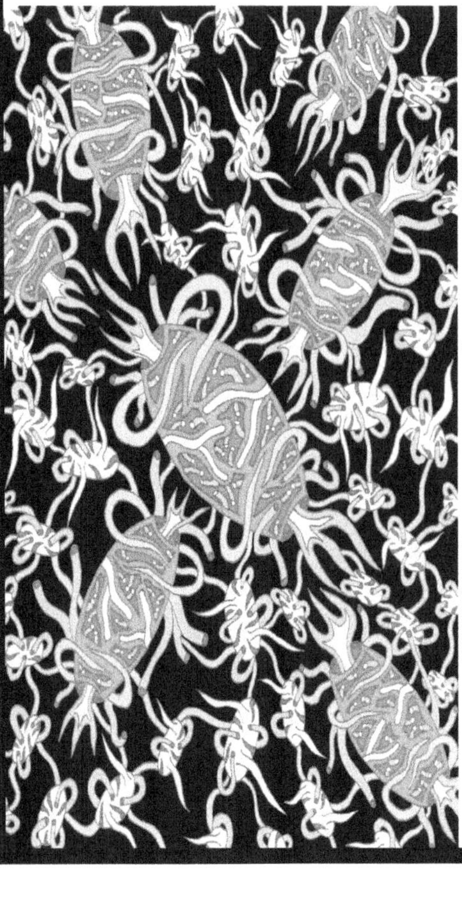
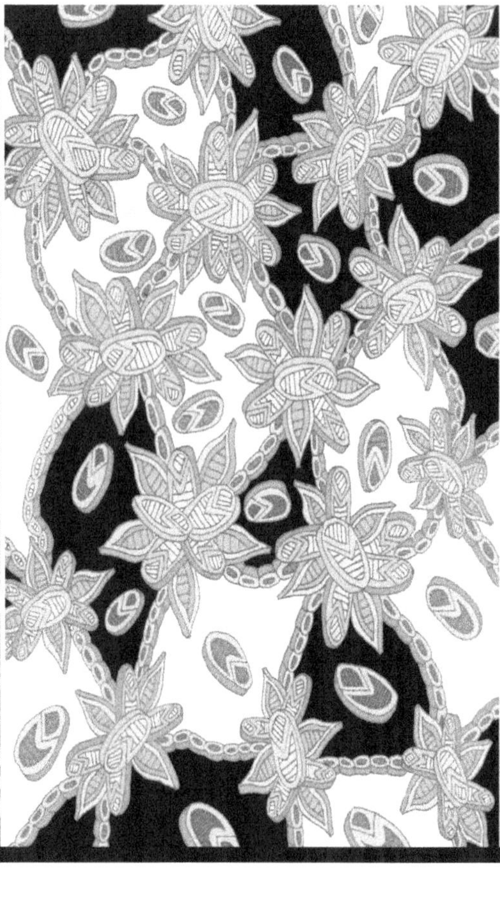
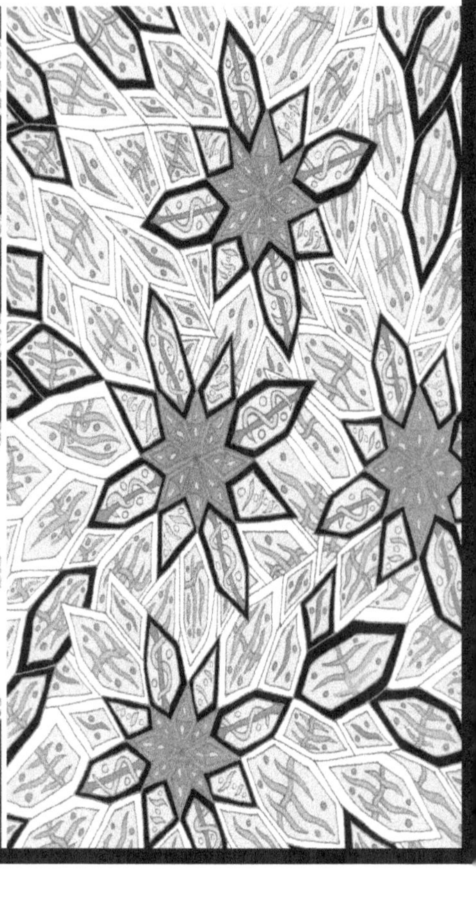

www.ingramcontent.com/pod-product-compliance
Lightning Source LLC
Chambersburg PA
CBHW080541190526
45169CB00007B/2590
* 9 7 8 1 5 3 3 0 5 6 2 0 7 *